JAN

Charlotte Brontë

AUTHORED by Masha Wasilewsky
UPDATED AND REVISED by Gemma Cooper-Novack

COVER DESIGN by Table XI Partners LLC
COVER PHOTO by Olivia Verma and © 2005 GradeSaver, LLC

BOOK DESIGN by Table XI Partners LLC

Published by GradeSaver LLC, www.gradesaver.com

First published in the United States of America by GradeSaver LLC. 2015

GRADESAVER, the GradeSaver logo and the phrase "Getting you the grade since 1999" are registered trademarks of GradeSaver, LLC

ISBN 978-1-60259-774-7

Printed in the United States of America

For other products and additional information please visit http://www.gradesaver.com

Table of Contents

Biography of Charlotte Bronte (1816–1855)

Charlotte Brontë was the third child of the Reverend Patrick Brontë and Maria Branwell. Born in 1816, Charlotte was soon followed by her brother Patrick Branwell in 1817, her sister Emily in 1818, and her sister Ann in 1820. The four siblings had an extremely close relationship, and their childhood collaboration would lead to a creative spirit unexpected from the children of an Anglican clergyman. In 1821, the family moved to Haworth in Yorkshire, where the Reverend had been appointed Perpetual Curate. Maria Branwell died of cancer in 1821, leaving five daughters and one son in the care of their somewhat severe father.

In 1824, Reverend Brontë had his four eldest daughters sent to study at the Clergy Daughter's School in Cowan Bridge. Conditions at the school were poor, and fever constantly broke out at the school. Throughout her life, Charlotte would attribute the school's poor conditions to the deaths of her sisters Maria and Elizabeth, both of whom succumbed to tuberculosis. After the death of their sisters, Charlotte, Emily, and Anne were withdrawn from the school and brought home, and the children's aunt, Elizabeth Branwell, became their new instructor.

Though the remaining children were deeply affected by the death of their two sisters, they filled their spare time with imaginative fantasies and fictitious worlds. For example, after their father gave Patrick Branwell a box of toy soldiers in 1826, the children were inspired to invent and write sagas about imaginary worlds called Angria and Gondal. Considering the bleak surroundings of the Yorkshire countryside, it is not surprising that the Bronte children began to explore their powers of imagination at an early age.

In 1831, Charlotte was sent to study at the Roe Head School, an institution headed by Mrs. Wooler and containing seven to ten additional students. Because of her father's declining health, it was particularly important for Charlotte to have enough of an education to be able to be economically independent. Charlotte's time at the Roe Head School was difficult: her Irish accent, uneven education, and quaint manner of dressing set her apart from the other pupils at the school, and she suffered from extreme homesickness. However, Mrs. Wooler was an encouraging teacher and helped Charlotte to overcome the limits of her previous education. Charlotte eventually earned several awards for outstanding scholarship, and, in 1832, was offered a position as a teacher at the school.

Charlotte declined the offer to teach at the Roe Head School in order to return home and instruct her sisters, over whom she now had educational advantages. The majority of Charlotte's time was spent studying with her sisters, teaching Sunday school classes, exploring the moors, and writing short fictional works. She also corresponded frequently with Ellen Nussey and Mary Taylor, both of whom she had met at the Roe Head school. In 1835, Charlotte returned to Mrs. Wooler's school to teach while her sister Emily accompanied her as a pupil. Emily soon left the school because of homesickness but was replaced by her sister Ann.

Three years later, Charlotte left the Roe Head School in order to assume a position as a governess to the Sidgewick family. Leaving her post after only three months, Charlotte returned to Haworth. In 1841, she took a post as governess to the White family but, again, left after only a few months. In 1842, Charlotte and Emily traveled to Brussels in order to complete their education at a pensionnat run by the schoolmaster Constantin Hegin and his wife -- and exchanged English and music lessons for board and tuition. After a brief trip back to Haworth, Charlotte returned alone to Brussels and became emotionally attached to Hegin. When Charlotte's love was not reciprocated, she became overwhelmed with depression and returned to Haworth in 1844.

Upon Charlotte's return, she and Emily realized their dream of opening a school in Haworth. Unfortunately, the school was a complete failure: the advertisements for the school did not result in a single public response. With the failure of the school, Charlotte and her sisters were free to focus on their literary careers. Having discovered some of Emily's poems during the previous year, Charlotte decided to publish selected poems of all three sisters; in 1846, a collection of their poems was published under the pseudonyms of Currer, Ellis, and Acton Bell. Charlotte's first novel, "The Professor," was also written during this time, though it was initially rejected for publication and was met with very little enthusiasm. However, Charlotte's second novel, "Jane Eyre," was published the following year and was a resounding success. The same year also saw the publication of Emily's novel "Wuthering Heights" and Ann's "Agnes Grey."

In 1848, Charlotte visited her publisher in London and revealed the true identity of the "Bells." However, her happiness at their literary success was soon marred by the death of her brother, Patrick, followed shortly by the deaths of both Emily and Ann. Charlotte coped with her loss by spending time within the literary circles of London, among such making figures such as William James Thackeray, and striving to edit her sisters' works. At this point, Charlotte began to suffer from health problems of her own.

In 1852, the Reverend Arthur Bell Nicholls, the curate of Haworth since 1845, proposed marriage to Charlotte. Unfortunately, Charlotte's father was violently opposed to the match, and Charlotte refused to accept the proposal. According to many accounts, Charlotte was not in love with the Reverend Nicholls and thus, was not overly heartbroken at her father's opposition. In the midst of this disappointed courtship, Charlotte worked on her next novel, "Villette," which was published in 1853. The following year, the Reverend Brontë's opposition to the Reverend Nicholls faded, and the Reverend Nicholls renewed his proposal to Charlotte. Despite her seeming apathy towards him, Charlotte married him in 1854. Shortly after becoming pregnant, she was diagnosed with pneumonia and died of the disease in 1855. She was only thirty-nine years old.

Some biographers claim that Charlotte Brontë actually starved herself to death because of her dislike of her husband. Others argue that her death was merely a subconscious effort to relieve herself of the depression that had plagued her entire life. Charlotte's personal life was ultimately an unhappy one, and, according to her contemporary biographer Elizabeth Gaskell, Charlotte never harbored any hope for the future. The settings and themes of her novels and poems demonstrate this sense of hopelessness and also highlight her belief that God had appointed some people for sorrow and some people for happiness. Although "Jane Eyre" can be read as a happy novel, the isolated mentality of the heroine and the difficult circumstances of her upbringing clearly reflect Charlotte's own perception of the world.

Teacher Guide - About the Author

Charlotte Brontë was the third child of the Reverend Patrick Brontë and Maria Branwell. Born in 1816, Charlotte was soon followed by her brother Patrick Branwell (called Branwell) in 1817, her sister Emily in 1818, and her sister Anne in 1820. The four siblings had an extremely close relationship, and their childhood collaboration would lead to a creative spirit unexpected from the children of an Anglican clergyman. In 1821, the family moved to Haworth in Yorkshire, where the Reverend had been appointed Perpetual Curate. Maria Branwell died of cancer in 1821, leaving five daughters and one son in the care of their somewhat severe father.

In 1824, Reverend Brontë had his four eldest daughters sent to study at the Clergy Daughter's School in Cowan Bridge. Conditions at the school were poor, and fever constantly broke out at the school. Throughout her life, Charlotte would attribute the deaths of her elder sisters Maria and Elizabeth, who succumbed to tuberculosis at the ages of eleven and twelve, to the school's poor conditions. After the death of their sisters, Charlotte, Emily, and Anne were withdrawn from the school and brought home, and the children's aunt, Elizabeth Branwell, became their new instructor.

Though the remaining children were deeply affected by the death of their two sisters, they filled their spare time with imaginative fantasies and fictitious worlds. For example, after their father gave Patrick Branwell a box of toy soldiers in 1826, the children were inspired to invent and write sagas about imaginary worlds called Angria (Charlotte and Branwell) and Gondal (Emily and Anne). Considering the bleak surroundings of the Yorkshire countryside, it is not surprising that the Brontë children began to explore their powers of imagination at an early age.

In 1831, Charlotte was sent to study at the Roe Head School, an institution headed by Mrs. Wooler and containing seven to ten additional students. Because of her father's declining health, it was particularly important for Charlotte to have enough of an education to be able to be economically independent. Charlotte's time at the Roe Head School was difficult: her Irish accent, uneven education, and quaint manner of dressing set her apart from the other pupils at the school, and she suffered from extreme homesickness. However, Mrs. Wooler was an encouraging teacher and helped Charlotte to overcome the limits of her previous education. Charlotte eventually earned several awards for outstanding scholarship, and, in 1832, was offered a position as a teacher at the school.

Charlotte declined the offer to teach at the Roe Head School in order to return home and instruct her sisters, over whom she now had educational advantages. The majority of Charlotte's time was spent studying with her sisters, teaching Sunday school classes, exploring the moors, and writing short fictional works. She also corresponded frequently with Ellen Nussey and Mary Taylor, both of whom she had met at the Roe Head school. In 1835, Charlotte returned to Mrs. Wooler's school to teach while her sister Emily accompanied her as a pupil. Emily soon left the school because of homesickness, but was replaced by her sister Anne.

Three years later, Charlotte left the Roe Head School in order to assume a position as a governess to the Sidgewick family. Leaving her post after only three months, Charlotte returned to Haworth. In 1841, she took a post as governess to the White family but, again, left after only a few months. In 1842, Charlotte and Emily traveled to Brussels in order to complete their education at a pensionnat run by the schoolmaster Constantin Hegin and his wife — and exchanged English and music lessons for board and tuition. After a brief trip back to Haworth, Charlotte returned alone to Brussels and became emotionally attached to Hegin. When Charlotte's love was not reciprocated, she was overwhelmed with depression and returned to Haworth in 1844.

Upon Charlotte's return, she and Emily worked to realize their dream of opening a school in Haworth. Unfortunately, the school was a complete failure: the advertisements for the school did not result in a single public response. With the failure of the school, Charlotte and her sisters were free to focus on their literary careers. Having discovered some of Emily's poems during the previous year, Charlotte decided to submit for publication the selected poems of all three sisters; in 1846, a collection of their poems was published under the pseudonyms of Currer, Ellis, and Acton Bell. Charlotte's first novel, *The Professor*, was also written during this time, though it was initially rejected for publication and was met with very little enthusiasm. However, Charlotte's second novel, *Jane Eyre*, was published the following year and was a resounding success. The same year also saw the publication of Emily's novel *Wuthering Heights* and Anne's *Agnes Grey*.

In 1848, Charlotte visited her publisher in London and revealed the true identity of the "Bells." However, her happiness at their literary success was soon marred by the death of her brother, Branwell, followed shortly by the deaths of both Emily and Anne. Charlotte coped with her loss by spending time within the literary circles of London, among such making figures such as William Makepeace Thackeray, and striving to edit her sisters' works. At this point, Charlotte began to suffer from health problems of her own.

In 1852, the Reverend Arthur Bell Nicholls, the curate of Haworth since 1845, proposed marriage to Charlotte. Unfortunately, Charlotte's father was violently opposed to the match, and Charlotte refused to accept the proposal. (According to many accounts, Charlotte was not in love with the Reverend Nicholls and thus, was not overly heartbroken at her father's opposition.) In the midst of this disappointed courtship, Charlotte worked on her next novel, *Villette*, which was published in 1853. The following year, the Reverend Brontë's opposition to the Reverend Nicholls faded, and the Reverend Nicholls renewed his proposal to Charlotte. Despite her seeming apathy towards him, Charlotte married him in 1854. Shortly after becoming pregnant, she was diagnosed with pneumonia and died of the disease in 1855. She was only thirty-nine years old.

Some biographers claim that Charlotte Brontë actually starved herself to death because of her dislike of her husband. Others argue that her death was merely a subconscious effort to relieve herself of the depression that had plagued her entire life. Charlotte's personal life was ultimately an unhappy one, and, according to her biographer and friend Elizabeth Gaskell, Charlotte never harbored any hope for the future. The settings and themes of her novels and poems demonstrate this sense of hopelessness and also highlight her belief that God had appointed some people for sorrow and some people for happiness. Although *Jane Eyre* can be read as a happy novel, the isolated mentality of the heroine and the difficult circumstances of her upbringing clearly reflect Charlotte's own perception of the world.

Teacher Guide - Study Objectives

If all of the elements of this lesson plan are employed, students will develop the following powers, skills, and understanding:

1. Students will be able to analyze and write about ideas and themes found in *Jane Eyre*.

2. Students will be able to apply ideas and themes from *Jane Eyre* to their own lives.

3. Students will be able to consider the motivations and inner workings of characters in *Jane Eyre*.

Teacher Guide - Common Core Standards

1. 11-12

    CCSS.ELA-Literacy.CCRA.R.1
    Read closely to determine what the text says explicitly and to make logical
    inferences from it; cite specific textual evidence when writing or speaking
    to support conclusions drawn from the text.

2. 11-12

    CCSS.ELA-Literacy.CCRA.R.2
    Determine central ideas or themes of a text and analyze their development;
    summarize the key supporting details and ideas.

3. 11-12

    CCSS.ELA-Literacy.CCRA.R.3
    Analyze how and why individuals, events, or ideas develop and interact
    over the course of a text.

4. 11-12

    CCSS.ELA-Literacy.CCRA.R.5
    Analyze the structure of texts, including how specific sentences,
    paragraphs, and larger portions of the text (e.g., a section, chapter, scene,
    or stanza) relate to each other and the whole.

5. 11-12

    CCSS.ELA-Literacy.CCRA.R.7
    Integrate and evaluate content presented in diverse media and formats,
    including visually and quantitatively, as well as in words.

6. 11-12

    CCSS.ELA-Literacy.CCRA.R.10
    Read and comprehend complex literary and informational texts
    independently and proficiently.

7. 11-12

    CCSS.ELA-Literacy.CCRA.W.3
    Write narratives to develop real or imagined experiences or events using
    effective technique, well-chosen details and well-structured event
    sequences.

8. 11-12

   <u>CCSS.ELA-Literacy.CCRA.W.6</u>
   Use technology, including the Internet, to produce and publish writing and to interact and collaborate with others.

9. 11-12

   <u>CCSS.ELA-Literacy.CCRA.SL.1</u>
   Prepare for and participate effectively in a range of conversations and collaborations with diverse partners, building on others' ideas and expressing their own clearly and persuasively.

10. 11-12

    <u>CCSS.ELA-Literacy.CCRA.SL.3</u>
    Evaluate a speaker's point of view, reasoning, and use of evidence and rhetoric.

11. 11-12

    <u>CCSS.ELA-Literacy.CCRA.SL.4</u>
    Present information, findings, and supporting evidence such that listeners can follow the line of reasoning and the organization, development, and style are appropriate to task, purpose, and audience.

12. 11-12

    <u>CCSS.ELA-Literacy.CCRA.SL.5</u>
    Make strategic use of digital media and visual displays of data to express information and enhance understanding of presentations.

Teacher Guide - Introduction to Jane Eyre

According to David Cody, Charlotte Brontë "wrote because writing provided her with a psychological release: life without composition was unthinkable to her. Full of manifestations of her sense of deprivation, tension, and repression, her creative work — intuitively, almost unconsciously — came more and more to provide her with a means of filling the time which spreads between me and the grave,' as one of her characters puts it" (Cody, 1). Cody writes: "In a very real sense Charlotte's life was spent in mourning, in a struggle against the grim realities which surrounded her — abandonment, brutalization, emotional deprivation, death (during her life she was forced to confront the traumatic loss of her mother, her four sisters, and her brother) and the search for reality, for her own identity" (Cody, 1).

About *Jane Eyre*'s protagonist, Charlotte Brontë wrote, "I will show you a heroine as plain and small as myself." In fact, elements of Charlotte Brontë's life are found in *Jane Eyre*. For example, the deadly typhus fever epidemic at Lowood mirrors some of Charlotte Brontë's school experiences. In 1824, she attended the Clergy Daughter's School with her sisters Maria, Elizabeth, and Emily. At school, Maria and Elizabeth got sick, were brought home, and died quickly. Emily and Charlotte were brought home shortly thereafter.

Charlotte Brontë published *Jane Eyre* in 1847 under the androgynous pseudonym of Currer Bell. *Jane Eyre* was well-received, and soon Charlotte Brontë was able to identify herself as a woman and reveal her real name. The revelation of Charlotte Brontë's true identity allowed *Jane Eyre* "to achieve an additional level of interest in contemporary society by forcing the public to redefine sexist notions of female authorship." Melissa Lowes writes: "In a time when women were considered little more than social adornments and bearers of offspring, Charlotte Brontë bravely contradicted society through her writing. Her novels speak volumes for the oppressed woman; thus establishing Charlotte Brontë as one of the first modern women of her time" (Lowes, 1). The text contains elements of the Gothic, such as the "Madwoman in the Attic" conceit, and Mr. Rochester has elements of the Byronic hero.

Jane Eyre has proven a timeless classic: it has been continuously successful since its publication, and has inspired many other books as well as several film adaptations.

Key Aspects of Jane Eyre

Tone

Over the course of the novel, Jane Eyre reflects back on her childhood, adolescence, and adult life. The book's tone is at times reflective, analytical, passionate, suspenseful, and mysterious.

Setting

The novel is set in England in the nineteenth century.

Point of view

The novel is framed as an autobiography, and is written from the point of view of its protagonist, Jane Eyre.

Character development

Jane Eyre: Jane is the novel's protagonist, and the novel is written from her point of view. Throughout her life, she faces and overcomes hardships by holding fast to her inner core of intelligence, kindness, courage, empathy, independence, and honesty. Jane begins the book as a shy, scared young girl; she becomes an adolescent who speaks her mind, a young woman blinded and then betrayed by love, and an adult woman possessed of hard-won resilience and wisdom, as well as passion and compassion.

Bessie: Bessie is the nurse who takes care of Jane at Mrs. Reed's house. She is the only person in the house who shows Jane even a modicum of kindness. Later, she marries and raises a family with Robert Leaven, Mrs. Reed's coachman, and maintains a friendship with Jane.

Mr. Rochester: Mr. Rochester is Jane's employer at Thornfield Hall, where she works as a governess after she leaves Lowood. At first proud and removed, he gradually falls in love with Jane, and sees in her the possibility of a new and happy life. He proposes to Jane even though he is already married, to a mad and violent woman whom he tries to confine to his attic, and he is nearly destroyed when Jane learns the truth and leaves him. Mr. Rochester's wife sets fire to Thornfield Hall, the second time burning it to the ground before plunging to her own death. Mr. Rochester rescues his household staff and tries to rescue his wife, too, and is blinded and injured in the process; this experience humbles him. Jane returns to his side to care for him, and he and Jane marry, restoring Mr. Rochester's hope for the future. He gradually regains sight in one of his eyes in time to see his first-born child.

Mrs. Reed: Mrs. Reed, Jane's guardian at the beginning of the novel, feels an antipathy for Jane that she carries with her adamantly until death. Mrs. Reed and her husband take Jane in after the death of Jane's parents, and she promises her husband when he dies that she will continue taking care of Jane. Mrs. Reed resents having made this promise, and relents only slightly when Jane visits Mrs. Reed at her deathbed and wants to reconcile

Mr. Brocklehurst: Mr. Brocklehurst runs Lowood. He tries to instill humility in the students at Lowood, but when his own daughters and wife appear at Lowood, they are lavishly dressed. He takes Mrs. Reed at her word that Jane is a liar, and publicly accuses Jane of being one when he first sees Jane at Lowoood. After an outbreak of typhus ravages the school, conditions at Lowood are examined and then changed for the better. Due to Mr. Brocklehurst's wealth and family connections, he cannot be completely removed from Lowood after its restructuring, but his duties at the school are supervised by people with a more humane view.

Blanche Ingram: Blanche Ingram is a beautiful, vivacious, and musically accomplished young woman who comes to visit Mr. Rochester as part of a gathering of guests. She and Mr. Rochester seem to be romantically interested in each other, although she seems to back off after she receives seemingly disturbing news from Mr. Rochester, disguised as a fortune-teller. Despite her outer beauty, she shows her inner emptiness in her disdainful and dismissive treatment of Adèle.

Helen Burns: Helen Burns is Jane's friend at Lowood. Both she and Jane love to read. Helen is constantly picked on by Mrs. Scatcherd, the History teacher at Lowood, but bears it with equanimity. Her accepting nature constrasts with Jane's, and Jane often feels angry on Helen Burns's behalf. Helen trusts Jane implicitly and helps Jane find her own inner compass when she is accused of lying. During the typhus epidemic at Lowood, Helen falls gravely ill with consumption, and Jane manages to visit her once before she dies.

Miss Temple: Miss Temple is Jane's mentor at Lowood. From Jane's first day, Jane can see how Miss Temple finds ways to show kindness, to try to make the students' time at Lowood less intolerable. She is reasonable, and gives Jane a way to exonerate herself when she is publicly accused of being a liar. Miss Temple eventually marries and leaves Lowood to move with her husband far away.

Eliza Reed: Eliza Reed enjoys participating in commerce as a child, and when Jane meets her later in life, Eliza still has that streak of practicality. Eliza longs to take her financial savings and separate herself from her family, living someplace where she can follow her strict daily schedule in peace. After Mrs. Reed's death, Eliza joins a convent in France.

Georgiana Reed: When Jane is a child living in Mrs. Reed's house, Georgiana Reed is generally thought of as the beauty, and Georgiana's appearance wins people over. Later in life, Georgiana still is fixated on her appearance and it is what she presents to the world as a thing she has worth appreciating. When Jane meets her as Mrs. Reed is dying, Georgiana is fixated on a previous social triumph in which she had been admired for her beauty. Georgiana escapes the Reed family's financial troubles by marrying advantageously.

John Reed: John torments Jane when they are children, and grows more dissipated as he grows older. Eventually, before his death, he squanders his family's money through gambling. Like the other Reed children, as John grows, his character hardens into a more extreme form of what it was when he was a child.

St. John Rivers: St. John Rivers is a minister who lives with his sisters, Diana and Mary. St. John is devoutly religious, controlling and rigid with himself and with others, filled with ambition and a yearning for adventure beyond the scope of his current life, and longs to be a missionary. He is in love with Rosamond Oliver, who loves him, too, but he wrestles with his feelings, afraid that a life with Rosamond Oliver would be too comfortable and complacent, and that it would preclude his being a missionary. She eventually marries someone else, and St. John proposes to Jane. Jane declines his proposal, and he goes to be a missionary in India without marrying.

Diana Rivers: Diana is well-educated and kind. She is empathetic towards Jane from the beginning of Jane's stay. She encourages Jane and St. John to get to know each other better, but also is supportive of Jane when Jane turns down St. John's marriage proposal. She works as a governess to make ends meet financially. She eventually marries a captain in the navy.

Mary Rivers: Like her sister, Mary is well-educated and kind, and is empathetic towards Jane. Also, like her sister, Mary works as a governess in order to keep afloat financially. Mary eventually marries a clergyman.

Mrs. Fairfax: Mrs. Fairfax is Mr. Rochester's housekeeper. Mrs. Fairfax is warm-hearted and reasonable, and she and Jane find an instant comfort in each other's company. When Jane and Mr. Rochester become engaged, Mrs. Fairfax, while expressing congratulations, also warns Jane to be careful. After Jane leaves and Mr. Rochester wants to be more isolated, he helps Mrs. Fairfax settle in with friends and provides her with an annuity.

Adèle Varens: Adèle is Mr. Rochester's ward, and also possibly his child. Mr. Rochester once had a love affair with Adèle's mother, a French opera-dancer, whom he supported financially and who turned out to be cheating on him. Unsure of Adèle's paternity, Mr. Rochester nonetheless takes in Adèle to be raised at Thornfield. Eventually, after Jane leaves, Adèle is sent to school by Mr. Rochester. When Jane returns, she first brings Adèle home from her school, which she and Adèle agree is too severe, and then finds another school for her, where Adèle can be happy and where Jane can visit Adèle often.

Bertha Mason: A beautiful woman from a prominent Creole family in the West Indies, Bertha Mason, encouraged by her family and Mr. Rochester's family, marries Mr. Rochester after knowing him a short time. Mr. Rochester does not know when he marries Bertha Mason that she ""came of a mad family." This soon shows itself, and her condition eventually deteriorates; she is kept by Mr. Rochester on the third floor of Thornfield Hall as she grows more and more violent. Near the end of the novel, Bertha sets fire to Thornfield Hall and perishes in the fire.

Themes

Internal vs. External Beauty: This is a conflict that is explored throughout the novel. One pair that highlights this conflict in *Jane Eyre* is Jane Eyre vs. Blanche Ingram. Blanche is outwardly beautiful and accomplished, but inwardly lacking in depth of thought or emotion. She seems to have captured Mr. Rochester's interest with her beauty and vivacity. However, it is Jane, with whom Mr. Rochester happily converses for hours and who treats Mr. Rochester's ward, Adèle, with kindness and empathy (contrasted with Blanche Ingram's harsh and disdainful treatment of Adèle), with whom Mr. Rochester is truly smitten.

Family: At the beginning of the novel, Jane is living with relatives (Mrs. Reed's husband is Jane's uncle), but is pointedly not treated like family. Throughout the novel, Jane makes discoveries about her family, and yearns for a sense of family connection. For instance, when she finds that Diana, St. John, and Mary Rivers are her cousins, and that the uncle from whom she inherits twenty thousand pounds is their uncle, too, but has left them a total of thirty guineas between them, Jane is happy to share her inheritance with them, both as a way to help them and as a way to show her gratitude for having the warmth and groundedness that family can provide.

Education: School provides Jane with an escape from life at Mrs. Reed's house, even if adjusting to school life at Lowood brings troubles of its own. Through Jane's time at Lowood, the novel explores the ramifications of different purposes and methods of education. The school's educational philosophy receives an overhaul after the outbreak of a deadly epidemic of typhus. Conditions for students improve, and the school's new philosophy balances academic rigor with empathy for students. The skills and knowledge Jane gains at Lowood provide her with a livelihood as well as means of connecting with others. Jane can find teaching employment, as a teacher or as a governess. Her knowledge of French allows her to communicate with Adèle, and her skill as an artist helps her to find common ground with others. For instance, offering to create portraits of Georgiana and Eliza, Mrs. Reed's daughters, helps break the ice when Jane returns to Mrs. Reed's house to see Mrs. Reed on her deathbed.

Love vs. Independence: Jane experiences this conflict in the novel. She tells Mr. Rochester, "I am no bird; and no net ensnares me; I am a free human being with an independent will, which I now exert to leave you." Other characters engage this conflict as well: St. John Rivers, for instance, wrestles to reconcile his love for Rosamond Oliver with his wish to become a missionary and travel far away. He believes that if he marries Rosamond Oliver, he will fall into a comfortable and complacent life with her that he will chafe against as he yearns for adventure, new places, and professional fulfillment.

Symbols

Landscape and Weather: Descriptions of landscapes and weather are used in the novel to either contrast or mirror Jane's mental state and actions. For instance, the description of Jane's gloomy time spent living with Mrs. Reed is mirrored by a description of gloomy, rainy weather. On the other hand, at Lowood, while winter leads to spring in a way that mirrors Jane's initial hardships at Lowood leading to an adjustment to the place (mirroring), the spring at Lowood also brings with it an outbreak of typhus fever (contrast). The depiction of a winter storm coming in

Biography of Charlotte Brontë (1816–1855)

summer illustrates Jane's emotional state after the discovery of Mr. Rochester's marital status.

Red Room: Jane is put into the red room, a room not often used in Mrs. Reed's house as it was the site of Mr. Reed's death, as a form of punishment. Being put in this room is traumatic for Jane, and represents her childhood experience with the Reeds.

The Attic: The attic, where Mr. Rochester keeps his mad wife, represents secrecy, separation, and misunderstanding. Many contemporary literary analyses use the image of the "madwoman in the attic" to connote fear of female power.

Fire: Fire represents passion in *Jane Eyre*. Both Jane and Rochester are described using fire imagery during the course of the book; Bertha Mason, who will ultimately burn down Thornfield, has no control over her fire, but is simply a being of untethered passion.

Climax

The climax of the novel arrives when St. John proposes to Jane and wants to take her to India. While considering St. John's proposal, Jane hears what she thinks is Mr. Rochester's voice calling her name, and leaves to go to Thornfield to search for him. At this point, the novel's conflicts begin to resolve. Mr. Rochester, whose wife died in the fire that she set that destroyed Thornfield, is alive, though injured and blind. They marry, Jane is happy to care for him, and, eventually, Mr. Rochester regains sight in one of his eyes. St. John does go off to India to pursue his dream of becoming a missionary, though he does not marry. Adèle and Mrs. Fairfax both end up settled in positive situations—Mrs. Fairfax with friends and with an annuity from Mr. Rochester and Adèle at a school where Jane can visit her. Mary and Diana Rivers both end up in happy marriages and keep in contact with Jane.

Structure

Jane Eyre is a novel containing thirty-nine chapters, split into three volumes. These lesson plans also include the Preface to the Second Edition and the Note to the Third Edition.

Teacher Guide - Relationship to Other Books

Jane Eyre: The Graphic Novel, an adaptation of Charlotte Brontë's text with script adaptation by Amy Corzin, artwork by John M. Burns, lettering by Terry Wiley, design and layout by Jo Wheeler, puts the story of *Jane Eyre* into a graphic novel format.

Wide Sargasso Sea by Jean Rhys is a prequel to *Jane Eyre* that tells an untold story of Mr. Rochester's first wife.

Charlotte Brontë worked closely with her sisters; Anne Brontë's *Agnes Grey* was published with *Jane Eyre*, and Emily Brontë's *Wuthering Heights* published shortly before. Anne's *The Tenant of Wildfell Hall* came out soon after, followed by Charlotte's *Villette*.

Teacher Guide - Bringing in Technology

Throughout the study of *Jane Eyre*, students with disabilities should have the option of using dictation software for writing assignments, and text-to-speech software for reading assignments.

On Day 1, students may use a document-sharing site for the "Characters' Diary Entries" activity.

Day 2's "Design Your Own School" activity can be taken in many directions, allowing students to make use of many different forms of technology, including design and presentation software and virtual modeling, in the design process as well as in the presentation process.

On Day 3, students will use a document-sharing site or a class blog for the "Building Suspense" activity.

Day 4's "Teacher-In-Role" activity could be presented online. They could also use digital illustration programs for the "Weather Imagery" activity.

On Day 5, students can create digital illustrations for *Jane Eyre* in addition to analog. They will also view the 2011 film adaptation of *Jane Eyre,* and will use the internet to look up reviews of the film.

Day 6's activity "Writing a Story Using a Pseudonym" can also utilize a class blog or document sharing.

Teacher Guide - Notes to the Teacher

Every classroom is different, but the in-depth character study and timeless themes in *Jane Eyre* may prove of interest to many adolescent students. These lessons and activities provide many different approaches to these themes; select those that best suit the strengths and interests of your own class. As a tie-in to *Jane Eyre*, it might be interesting to explore the lives of the Brontës. There is material from Charlotte Brontë's life found in the novel, and studying the lives and works of her and her family can provide historical context for the events in the novel.

The thought questions in this lesson plan provide material and ideas that students can use to write short original essays and to develop their powers of analysis.

The questions provided for the final paper are most suitable for student essays. For the sake of improving their written expression, of expression, teachers should encourage students to write on topics that have been discussed in class, this time in the more formal writing style expected in a literary essay. At the same time, students should not be discouraged from choosing their own topics. Remember that grading an essay should not depend on a simple checklist of required content, but should take a holistic approach to understanding. Use the rubric provided.

Biography of Charlotte Bronte (1816–1855)

Teacher Guide - Related Links

The Victorian Web

http://www.victorianweb.org

This website contains information about *Jane Eyre,* about Charlotte Brontë, and about the Victorian era, in general.

Haworth Village

http://www.haworth-village.org.uk/brontes/bronte.asp

This is the website of Haworth, where the Brontë family lived at Haworth Parsonage from 1820 to 1861. It has a section dedicated to the Brontë family's lives and works.

The Brontë Society & Brontë Parsonage Museum

http://www.bronte.org.uk/haworth-and-the-brontes/family-and-friends/charlotte-bronte

This site includes information about the Brontë Society, the Brontë Parsonage Museum, the Brontës' lives and works, information about the Brontë's creative legacy, and educational resources.

Teacher Guide - Jane Eyre Bibliography

Masha Wasilewsky, author of Lesson Plan. Completed on March 5, 2015, copyright held by GradeSaver.

Updated and revised by Gemma Cooper-Novack March 5, 2015. Copyright held by GradeSaver.

Brontë, Charlotte. Jane Eyre. New York, NY: Barnes & Noble Books, 2003.

Corzine, Amy; Burns, John M.; Wiley, Terry; Wheeler, Jo; Bryant, Clive. Jane Eyre: The Graphic Novel. Litchborough, Towcester: Classical Comics Ltd, 2008.

Rhys, Jean. Wide Sargasso Sea. New York, NY: André Deutsch (UK) & W. W. Norton (US), 1966.

Jane Eyre. Dir.Cary Joji Fukunagal. Perf. Wasikowska, Mia; Fassbender, Michael; Dench, Judi; Bell, Jamie. Ruby Films, 2011. Film.

Brontë, Charlotte, & Townsend, F.H. (Illustrator). "The Project Gutenberg eBook, Jane Eyre." David Price, email ccx074@pglaf.org. 4/29/2007. 11/24/2014. <http://www.gutenberg.org/files/1260/1260-h/1260-h.htm>.

Cody, David. "Charlotte Brontë: An Appreciation." The Victorian Web. 1987. 1/17/15. <http://www.victorianweb.org/authors/bronte/cbronte/brontbio1.html>.

Lowes, Melissa. "Charlotte Brontë: A Modern Woman." The Victorian Web. 2008. 1/18/2015. <http://www.victorianweb.org/authors/bronte/cbronte/lowes1.html>.

Day 1 - Reading Assignment, Questions, Vocabulary

Read *Jane Eyre,* Chapters I-VIII. (These chapters can be split up as needed between reading in class and reading at home.)

Common Core Objectives

- CCSS.ELA-LITERACY.RL.11-12.2
  Determine two or more themes or central ideas of a text and analyze their development over the course of the text, including how they interact and build on one another to produce a complex account; provide an objective summary of the text.

- CCSS.ELA-Literacy.W.11-12.3
  Write narratives to develop real or imagined experiences or events using effective technique, well-chosen details, and well-structured event sequences.

- CCSS.ELA-Literacy.W.11-12.6
  Use technology, including the Internet, to produce, publish, and update individual or shared writing products in response to ongoing feedback, including new arguments or information.

Note that it is perfectly fine to expand any day's work into two days depending on the characteristics of the class, particularly if the class will engage in all of the suggested classroom exercises and activities and discuss all of the thought questions.

Content Summary for Teachers

Chapter I

At the beginning of the novel, Jane is ten years old and living with Mrs. Reed and Mrs. Reed's three children, Eliza, Georgiana, and John. The Reeds all exclude Jane, and when Jane is forced to leave the company of Mrs. Reed and the other children for the day and goes to read alone, which is one of her only pleasures in the household, fourteen-year-old John finds her and provokes her, telling her that she has no right to read books in the house because she is dependent on the family, whereas he will inherit the house as an adult. When he physically attacks her, she fights back, and is immediately punished by being sent to the red-room.

Chapter II

Before Bessie and Miss Abbot lock Jane into the red-room, in which Mr. Reed died, they tell Jane that she should try to be more agreeable to Mrs. Reed because, if Mrs. Reed turns her out, she will go to the poorhouse. Jane ponders why she feels so unloved and out of place in the house, and why the ill-behaved Reeds are so beloved—she is sure that Mr. Reed, who was her uncle, would have treated her well had he lived. She then frightens herself with the idea that he might come back from beyond the grave, sees a frightening flash of light, and screams, begging to be taken out of the room. Bessie, Miss Abbot, and Mrs. Reed come to her, and Mrs. Reed says she will extend Jane's punishment because she disturbed them. Jane faints from the distress.

Chapter III

Jane wakes up in her own bed, attended by Mr. Lloyd, an apothecary, and Bessie, who is treating her more kindly. and singing a sad song that awakens Jane's melancholy for her orphaned state. Mr. Lloyd elicits from Jane the information that she is not happy in the home of Mrs. Reed, and asks her if she might want to attend school. She considers the idea, and ultimately decides that she would like to go to school. Jane later catches hints that a conversation about school for her has transpired between Mr. Lloyd and Mrs. Reed. She also learns, from overhearing Bessie and Miss Abbot's conversations, Jane's grandfather had disapproved of his daughter's marriage to Jane's father, a clergyman without much money, and had cut Jane's mother off financially. Then, a year into their marriage, Jane's father contracted typhus fever while caring for the poor; Jane's mother, too, contracted the disease, and both died "within a month of each other."

Chapter IV

While Jane convalesces, the Reed girls avoid her. John, however, continues to provoke her; when she fights back, his mother tells him that Jane is not worthy of associating with them. Jane, feeling as if she cannot control her own speech, responds that they are not worthy of associating with Jane, and says that the late Mr. Reed and her parents, watching from heaven, condemn the way Mrs. Reed treats Jane. Mrs. Reed boxes Jane's ears, and Bessie speaks against Jane as well.

Jane is excluded from holiday festivities at Gateshead, and then, in January, she is introduced to Mr. Brocklehurst, head of the Lowood school. After some uncomfortable interrogation about Jane's reading habits and piety, Mr. Brocklehurst accepts Jane as a student—but Mrs. Reed warns Mr. Brocklehurst that Jane tends to be deceitful. When he departs, Jane accuses Mrs. Reed of being more deceitful than she, and of being cruel; she declares that she will tell the world of Mrs. Reed's unjust and unkind treatment and will cut off contact with her when she goes to school. Bessie comforts Jane and helps her get ready for Lowood; she notes a change for the bolder in Jane's tone and demeanor.

Chapter V

Jane says goodbye to Bessie and travels to school. She arrives, is met by Miss Miller and another woman, who later turns out to be Miss Temple, the superintendent of Lowood. The next day, Jane begins the daily school routine with the other students. She is exhausted from hunger and thirst and looks forward to breakfast, which turns out to be burned porridge. Later in the day, Miss Temple orders bread and cheese for everyone.

Jane learns from a fellow student that the school is called Lowood Institution because it is "partly a charity-school"—the school educates students who are orphans or who have one parent who is dead. She also learns that Mr. Brocklehurst, whose mother is responsible for refurbishing part of the school, directs and oversees the school, and that everyone, including Miss Temple, reports to him. Later, Jane sees the same girl punished by Miss Scatcherd, the History teacher, by being made to stand in the middle of the school-room and wonders how the girl can bear the punishment without embarrassment.

Chapter VI

Jane continues to endure the difficult conditions at Lowood the next day. In History class, Miss Scatcherd focuses on the girl Jane met the previous day, Helen Burns, and though Helen manages to answer every question she is given, Miss Scatcherd continues to criticize her, and later beats her. When they converse, Helen tells Jane that she bears Miss Scatcherd's abuse because it is her duty, but that Miss Temple is a kinder teacher. Jane thinks that people should only be good to people who are good to them. Helen disagrees, even when Jane tells her about the Reeds, and states that Christ says "love your enemies" and that life is too short to nurse animosities—one should return kindness even for unkindness.

Chapter VII

During Jane's first quarter at Lowood, the students suffer from cold and hunger, although Miss Temple enhances their rations when she can. Mr. Brocklehurst pays a visit, telling Miss Temple that she ought not provide extra food for the students, and commenting that modesty and sobriety in appearance and the endurance of hardships are essential to a Lowood education. His wife and daughters, however, are lavishly dressed. Jane accidentally drops her slate and breaks it; Mr. Brocklehurst makes Jane stand on a stool, announces that Jane is a liar, and states that she should spend another half-hour on the stool and that nobody should speak to her for the rest of the day. At first, Jane is mortified, but then Helen smiles up at her, and Jane feels buoyed up and filled with Helen's strength.

Chapter VIII

Jane asks Helen how Helen can associate with somebody whom "everybody believes to be a liar." Helen answers that, first of all, only eighty people out of all of the people in the world even heard the accusation, and many dislike Mr. Brocklehurst; also, as long as Jane's conscience is at peace, it doesn't matter what other people think. Miss Temple finds Jane and Helen and invites them to her apartment for tea. Jane tells her about the Reeds, and Miss Temple states that she will write to Mr. Lloyd to publicly clear Jane of being a liar, but she believes Jane already. She then asks after Helen's health; Helen enjoys discussing history, books, and languages with Miss Temple, and Jane enjoys listening.

Helen and Jane return from Miss Temple's apartment to find Miss Scatcherd examining Helen's messy cupboard. The next day, Miss Scatcherd makes Helen wear a sign with "Slattern" written on it. After Miss Scatcherd's departure, Jane throws Helen's sign into the fire. When Mr. Lloyd responds to Miss Temple's letter and corroborates Jane's statements, Miss Temple makes a public announcement exonerating Jane. Jane then feels accepted by her teachers and peers and begins to flourish in her classes.

Thought Questions (students consider while they read)

1. In what does Jane find comfort during her time living with the Reeds?

2. How does Mrs. Reed feel about Jane?

3. Does Mr. Brocklehurst truly believe his own rhetoric about education?

4. What brings Helen and Jane together as friends?

5. How does Miss Temple function within Lowood?

Vocabulary (in order of appearance)

Chapter I: ...the cold winter wind had brought with it clouds so sombre, and a rain so penetrating, that further out-door exercise was now out of the question.

sombre:

gloomy, lacking brightness

Chapter I: near a scene of wet lawn and storm-beat shrub, with ceaseless rain sweeping away wildly before a long and lamentable blast.

ceaseless:

without end

lamentable:

regrettably bad, unfortunate, full of sorrow

Chapter I: The words in these introductory pages connected themselves with the succeeding vignettes, and gave significance to the rock standing up alone in a sea of billow and spray; to the broken boat stranded on a desolate coast; to the cold and ghastly moon glancing through bars of cloud at a wreck just sinking.

vignettes:

short descriptions or portrayals, small illustrations with edges that blend with what's outside of the illustrations

desolate:

lonely, empty, deserted

ghastly:

looking like a ghost, shockingly horrible, deathly pale

Chapter I: "It is well I drew the curtain," thought I; and I wished fervently he might not discover my hiding-place...

fervently:

with strong emotion, extremely enthusiastically

Chapter I: John had not much affection for his mother and sisters, and an antipathy to me.

antipathy:

a strong feeling of dislike

Chapter II: This reproach of my dependence had become a vague sing-song in my ear: very painful and crushing, but only half intelligible.

reproach:

expression of disapproval

Chapter II: This room was chill, because it seldom had a fire...

seldom:

hardly ever

Chapter II: Her beauty, her pink cheeks and golden curls, seemed to give delight to all who looked at her, and to purchase indemnity for every fault.

indemnity:

protection against loss, damage, or injury

Chapter II: What a consternation of soul was mine that dreary afternoon!

consternation:

a feeling of uneasiness, dread, confusion, or fear

Chapter II: How all my brain was in tumult, and all my heart in insurrection!

tumult:

commotion, agitation of feeling or mind

insurrection:

rebellion

Chapter II: I know that had I been a sanguine, brilliant, careless, exacting, handsome, romping child—though equally dependent and friendless—Mrs. Reed would have endured my presence more complacently...

sanguine:

cheerful, confident

Chapter II: I know that had I been a sanguine, brilliant, careless, exacting, handsome, romping child—though equally dependent and friendless—Mrs. Reed would have endured my presence more complacently;

endured:

tolerated

complacently:

contentedly, in an unconcerned way

Chapter II: I can now conjecture readily that this streak of light was, in all likelihood, a gleam from a lantern carried by some one across the lawn

conjecture:

make an inference or guess based on incomplete evidence

Chapter II: "What is all this?" demanded another voice peremptorily

peremptorily:

urgent, commanding, not allowing contradiction, putting an end to all action or debate

Chapter II: I was a precocious actress in her eyes; she sincerely looked on me as a compound of virulent passions, mean spirit, and dangerous duplicity.

precocious:

unusually advanced in talent, mental aptitude, or maturity

virulent:

poisonous, causing infection, hateful

Chapter III: The good apothecary appeared a little puzzled.

apothecary:

pharmacist

Chapter III: "I should indeed like to go to school," was the audible conclusion of my musings.

audible:

able to be heard

musings:

thoughts or reflections

Chapter IV: From my discourse with Mr. Lloyd, and from the above reported conference between Bessie and Abbot, I gathered enough of hope to suffice as a motive

for wishing to get well: a change seemed near,—I desired and waited it in silence.

discourse:

spoken or written communication

suffice:

be enough

Chapter IV: It tarried, however: days and weeks passed...

tarried:

stayed longer than intended, delayed

Chapter IV: What a miserable little poltroon had fear, engendered of unjust punishment, made of me in those days!

poltroon:

coward

engendered:

caused, brought about

Chapter IV: ...the vehement ringing of the breakfast-room bell decided me...

vehement:

forceful, intense, with strong feeling

Chapter IV: The action was more frank and fearless than any I was habituated to indulge in: somehow it pleased her.

habituated:

accustomed to

Chapter V: I only know that the day seemed to me of a preternatural length, and that we appeared to travel over hundreds of miles of road.

preternatural:

beyond of what is natural or normal

Chapter V: Ravenous, and now very faint, I devoured a spoonful or two of my portion without thinking of its taste...

ravenous:

extremely hungry

Chapter VI: ...I could distinguish from the gleeful tumult within, the disconsolate moan of the wind outside.

disconsolate:

hopelessly unhappy, without comfort or consolation

Chapter VI: ... when I should be listening to Miss Scatcherd, and collecting all she says with assiduity, often I lose the very sound of her voice; I fall into a sort of dream.

assiduity:

careful and constant attention or effort

Chapter VII: ...I have swallowed the remainder with an accompaniment of secret tears, forced from me by the exigency of hunger.

exigency:

urgent need or demand

Chapter VII: I can remember Miss Temple walking lightly and rapidly along our drooping line, her plaid cloak, which the frosty wind fluttered, gathered close about her, and encouraging us, by precept and example, to keep up our spirits, and march forward, as she said, "like stalwart soldiers."

precept:

a general rule or principle

stalwart:

loyal, dedicated, hardworking, reliable

Chapter VII: A little solace came at tea-time, in the shape of a double ration of bread—a whole, instead of a half, slice—with the delicious addition of a thin scrape of butter: it was the hebdomadal treat to which we all looked forward from Sabbath to Sabbath.

hebdomadal:

weekly

Chapter VIII: Miss Temple had smiled approbation...

approbation:

praise or approval

Chapter VIII: ...and if you persevere in doing well, these feelings will ere long appear so much the more evidently for their temporary suppression.

persevere:

continue with something despite difficulty

Chapter VIII: "If all the world hated you, and believed you wicked, while your own conscience approved you, and absolved you from guilt, you would not be without friends."

absolved:

freed from guilt, obligation, or blame

Chapter VIII: About a week subsequently to the incidents above narrated, Miss Temple, who had written to Mr. Lloyd, received his answer: it appeared that what he said went to corroborate my account.

corroborate:

validate, confirm, give support to

Additional Homework

1. Choose a character from *Jane Eyre* that we have encountered in the first eight chapters of the novel. What do you think will happen next in this character's life? Why do you think so? Write 2-3 paragraphs exploring these thoughts.

Day 1 - Discussion of Thought Questions

1. In what does Jane find comfort during her time living with the Reeds?

Time:

5 minutes

Discussion:

Jane finds solace in Bessie's songs and stories; Bessie shows her kindness that the Reed family members do not. Jane also derives some pleasure from reading, despite John's protests. Some students may also observe Jane's keen desire to be part of a family, and that having some sense of it is better than none.

2. How does Mrs. Reed feel about Jane?

Time:

10 minutes

Discussion:

Some students may think that Mrs. Reed treats Jane poorly because she resents being saddled with having to take care of Jane. Others may think that there is an underlying clash of personalities between Mrs. Reed and Jane that affects the way Mrs. Reed treats Jane. Students may also believe that Mrs. Reed is simply inclined to treat poorly those who are vulnerable or dependent. Mrs. Reed's attitude towards Jane shifts slightly when Jane is about to leave for school and when Jane states that she will tell anyone who will listen about Mrs. Reed's treatment of her—at this point, Mrs. Reed communicates with Jane almost as with an adult equal. To some students, this may indicate respect; to others, it will indicate that Mrs. Reed still dislikes Jane, but is inclined to protect herself.

3. Does Mr. Brocklehurst truly believe his own rhetoric about education?

Time:

10 minutes

Discussion:

Most students will probably think that he does not, since his standards for his daughters seem to be completely different from those he has for the students at his school. On the other hand, he may somehow be oblivious to his own hypocrisy. He may also believe that the students who are sent to his school are in need, somehow, of a form of guidance and upbringing that his own children do not require. He may also just enjoy his own power.

4. What brings Helen and Jane together as friends?

Time:

5 minutes

Discussion:

Both girls love reading, and sometimes look to it as a means of withdrawing from and/or the world. Also, they have similar feeling about Miss Scatcherd vs. Miss Temple, although Helen is more philosophical about the underlying merits behind Miss Scatcherd's treatment of her, and is committed to returning all treatment with kindness. Jane draws strength from Helen's composure and resilience, and Jane acts on emotions concerning Helen's treatment that Helen does not let herself experience. They share common interests, and complement each other.

5. How does Miss Temple function within Lowood?

Time:

5 minutes

Discussion:

While Miss Temple generally upholds and adheres to the school's guidelines, she also steps in to provide humane treatment of the students when she can (e.g. providing bread and butter for the students when the porridge is burned) and teaches her classes in a humane and judicious fashion. For Jane, Miss Temple represents the most positive aspects of education.

Day 1 - Short Answer Evaluation

1. After the girls at Lowood have to eat burned porridge, what does Miss Temple provide for the girls later in the day?

   _____

2. What happens after Miss Scatcherd examines Helen's belongings?

   _____

3. Of what is Jane publicly accused by Mr. Brocklehurst?

   _____

4. What are the names of Mrs. Reed's children?

   _____

5. Why does Jane live with Mrs. Reed at the beginning of the novel?

   _____

6. Who is Mr. Lloyd?

   _____

7. Who is Jane's first friend at Lowood?

   _____

8. What role does Mr. Brocklehurst play at Lowood?

   _____

9. How does John Reed treat Jane?

10. How are Georgiana and Eliza different from one another?

Answer Key

1. Miss Temple provides the girls with bread and butter.
2. Miss Scatcherd makes Helen wear a sign with the word "Slattern" written on it.
3. She is accused of being a liar.
4. Their names are Georgiana, Eliza, and John.
5. Mrs. Reed's husband, Jane's uncle, made her promise to take care of Jane because Jane's parents both died of typhus fever.
6. He is the apothecary who takes care of Jane, who first suggest to Jane the idea of going to school, and who later corroborates statements Jane makes to Miss Temple, leading Jane to be cleared of lying.
7. Jane's first friend at Lowood is Helen Burns.
8. He is the director of the school.
9. He teases her and tries to attack her, but withdraws behind his mother and accuses Jane of attacking him.
10. Eliza enjoys taking care of chickens, selling eggs, and generally participating in commerce. Georgiana is very beautiful and enjoys dressing nicely and doing her hair.

Day 1 - Crossword Puzzle

ACROSS

1. Short descriptions or portrayals, small illustrations with edges that blend with what's outside of the illustrations
3. A general rule or principle
5. Weekly
8. Accustomed to
9. Coward
12. Praise or approval
14. Loyal, dedicated, hardworking, reliable
15. Careful and constant attention or effort
17. At the beginning of the novel, Jane lives in the home of Mrs. _____
18. John Reed has sisters named Eliza and _____
19. Forceful, intense, with strong feeling

DOWN

2. The superintendent of Lowood, liked by Jane, is named Miss _____
3. Beyond what is natural or normal
4. A strong feeling of dislike
6. Urgent need or demand
7. Hopelessly unhappy, without comfort or consolation
10. Extremely hungry
11. Jane's school is called _____.
13. Continue with something despite difficulty
16. Gloomy, lacking brightness

Crossword Puzzle Answer Key

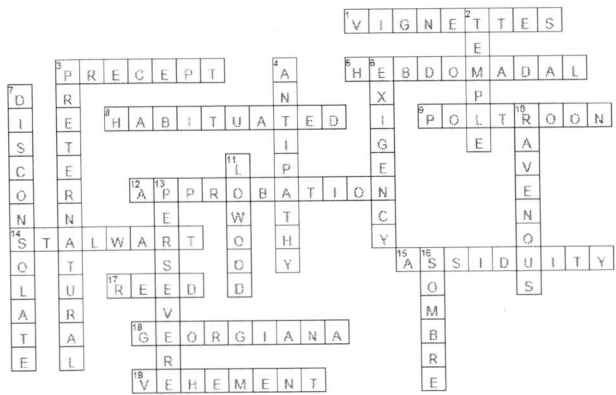

ACROSS

1. Short descriptions or portrayals, small illustrations with edges that blend with what's outside of the illustrations
3. A general rule or principle
5. Weekly
8. Accustomed to
9. Coward
12. Praise or approval
14. Loyal, dedicated, hardworking, reliable
15. Careful and constant attention or effort
17. At the beginning of the novel, Jane lives in the home of Mrs. _____.
18. John Reed has sisters named Eliza and _____
19. Forceful, intense, with strong feeling

DOWN

2. The superintendent of Lowood, liked by Jane, is named Miss _____
3. Beyond what is natural or normal
4. A strong feeling of dislike
6. Urgent need or demand
7. Hopelessly unhappy, without comfort or consolation
10. Extremely hungry
11. Jane's school is called _____.
13. Continue with something despite difficulty
16. Gloomy, lacking brightness

Day 1 - Vocabulary Quiz

Terms

1. _____ sombre
2. _____ lamentable
3. _____ desolate
4. _____ ghastly
5. _____ antipathy
6. _____ reproach
7. _____ seldom
8. _____ tumult
9. _____ indemnity
10. _____ fervently
11. _____ ceaseless
12. _____ complacently
13. _____ audible
14. _____ musings
15. _____ suffice
16. _____ habituated
17. _____ ravenous
18. _____ absolved
19. _____ corroborate
20. _____ approbation

Answers

A. accustomed to
B. commotion, agitation of feeling or mind
C. contentedly, in an unconcerned way
D. hardly ever
E. praise or approval
F. looking like a ghost, shockingly horrible, deathly pale
G. regrettably bad, unfortunate, full of sorrow
H. lonely, empty, deserted
I. thoughts or reflections
J. protection against loss, damage, or injury
K. be enough
L. validate, confirm, give support to
M. gloomy, lacking brightness
N. expression of disapproval
O. a strong feeling of dislike
P. with strong emotion, extremely enthusiastically
Q. extremely hungry
R. freed from guilt, obligation, or blame
S. able to be heard
T. without end

Answer Key

1. M sombre: gloomy, lacking brightness
2. G lamentable: regrettably bad, unfortunate, full of sorrow
3. H desolate: lonely, empty, deserted
4. F ghastly: looking like a ghost, shockingly horrible, deathly pale
5. O antipathy: a strong feeling of dislike
6. N reproach: expression of disapproval
7. D seldom: hardly ever
8. B tumult: commotion, agitation of feeling or mind
9. J indemnity: protection against loss, damage, or injury
10. P fervently: with strong emotion, extremely enthusiastically
11. T ceaseless: without end
12. C complacently: contentedly, in an unconcerned way
13. S audible: able to be heard
14. I musings: thoughts or reflections
15. K suffice: be enough
16. A habituated: accustomed to
17. Q ravenous: extremely hungry
18. R absolved: freed from guilt, obligation, or blame
19. L corroborate: validate, confirm, give support to
20. E approbation: praise or approval

l - Classroom Activities

e Your Own Autobiography

Kind of Activity:

Individual Writing

Objective:

Students will consider what events they think are worth remembering in a life by writing their own autobiographies.

Common Core Standards:

CCSS.ELA-LITERACY.RL.11-12.2; CCSS.ELA-Literacy.W.11-12.3

Time:

45 minutes

Structure:

1. *Jane Eyre* is presented as an autobiography of its main character. In pairs, students should brainstorm a list of events in her life that might be included in the novel—not just events that you have read about thus far, but events that you could imagine occurring in Jane's future. What are the typical milestones of a person's life? Does Jane seem like a typical person? Students should then reconvene as a class and pairs should share their lists with the class as a whole.

2. In preparation for reading the rest of the novel, students should write their own autobiographies. Students can create Life Graphs of their own lives to prepare for the writing process; this activity can help students gauge what they find important about their own lives—in positive ways and in negative ways. They should use their graphs to strenghten their planning and writing, looking back over their lives so far and creating a coherent narrative from their memories.

Ideas for Differentiated Instruction:

This activity can be modified for short- or long-term work: students could write just one autobiographical essay, in the style of one or two chapters in *Jane Eyre*, or they can continue adding to and modifying their autobiographies for the duration of the unit, perhaps being inspired by the content of the novel as they read on.

Assessment Ideas:

The autobiographies can be collected and graded for:

-grammar and mechanics

-effort, insight, and detail

2. Characters' Diary Entries

Kind of Activity:

Individual Writing

Objective:

Students will write diary entries from several characters' points of view.

Common Core Standards:

CCSS.ELA-LITERACY.RL.11-12.2; CCSS.ELA-Literacy.W.11-12.3; CCSS.ELA-Literacy.W.11-12.6

Time:

30 minutes

Structure:

1. As a class, students will list events that have happened in the novel so far. After coming up with events, students will list all of the characters that they can think of who are involved in each of the events. Who were the key players, and who were simply observers?

2. Individually, each student should choose one of the events discussed, and write diary entries from the points of view of each of the characters involved. In preparation, the students can create charts with rows for events in the novel and columns for characters. In each box where an event and a character meet, students can write details about how the character was involved in the event.

3. After the students write the diary entries, the students can share out, in groups or as a class, with a few students reading their diary entries for a particular character about a particular event. You could also create several shared documents to which all diary entries from a given character could be uploaded—e.g. "Jane's Diary," "Helen's Diary," "Mrs. Reed's Diary."

Ideas for Differentiated Instruction:

Students might also work collaboratively, with groups focusing on one event, each member of the group writing from a different character's point of view.

More advanced students could be encouraged to experiment with form—for example, writing dramatic scripts and monologues.

Assessment Ideas:

The diary entries can be graded for:

-grammar and mechanics

-effort and creativity

-understanding of characters

Day 2 - Reading Assignment, Questions, Vocabulary

Read *Jane Eyre,* Chapters IX-XVI. (These chapters can be split up as needed between reading in class and reading at home.)

Common Core Objectives

- CCSS.ELA-LITERACY.RL.11-12.2
  Determine two or more themes or central ideas of a text and analyze their development over the course of the text, including how they interact and build on one another to produce a complex account; provide an objective summary of the text.

- CCSS.ELA-Literacy.SL.11-12.1
  Initiate and participate effectively in a range of collaborative discussions (one-on-one, in groups, and teacher-led) with diverse partners on grades 11-12 topics, texts, and issues, building on others' ideas and expressing their own clearly and persuasively.

- CCSS.ELA-Literacy.SL.11-12.4
  Present information, findings, and supporting evidence, conveying a clear and distinct perspective, such that listeners can follow the line of reasoning, alternative or opposing perspectives are addressed, and the organization, development, substance, and style are appropriate to purpose, audience, and a range of formal and informal tasks.

- CCSS.ELA-Literacy.SL.11-12.5
  Make strategic use of digital media (e.g., textual, graphical, audio, visual, and interactive elements) in presentations to enhance understanding of findings, reasoning, and evidence and to add interest.

Note that it is perfectly fine to expand any day's work into two days depending on the characteristics of the class, particularly if the class will engage in all of the suggested classroom exercises and activities and discuss all of the thought questions.

Content Summary for Teachers

Chapters IX

In April, Spring comes to Lowood and life becomes less difficult. However, in May, there is also an outbreak of typhus at the school, and the neglect of the girls' health and nutrition causes most students to come down with the illness. Many die, either at school or after going home. The students who are unafflicted have more freedom and, as a result of Mr. Brocklehurst's distance from the school and the hiring of a new housekeeper, more food. Jane spends time with another friend, Mary Ann Wilson. Helen is ill with consumption and is being held somewhere separate from the students with typhus. Jane finds where Helen is and stays with her the night that she dies.

Chapter X

The typhus epidemic brings much-needed attention to the living conditions of the students at Lowood, and many improvements are made. Because of Mr. Brocklehurst's family connections and wealth, he stays on as treasurer and continues to conduct inspections at the school, but he works with people who are more generous and empathetic to the students' needs. The school becomes "in time a truly useful and noble institution" and Jane stays there for eight years—six as a student and then two as a teacher. Miss Temple continues to be Jane's mentor and friend, and Jane feels unsettled when Miss Temple marries and moves far away from Lowood with her husband. However, along with this unsettled feeling comes a sense that there is a wider world beyond Lowood's boundaries.

Jane puts out an advertisement in search of a position teaching children in a private family situation. She receives a response from Mrs. Fairfax of Thornfield, near Millcote describing a position teaching a little girl less than ten years old. Jane finds herself imagining what Mrs. Fairfax, Millcote, and Thornfield might be like. She takes a month to make arrangements with her new superintendent at Lowood, and Mrs. Fairfax, satisfied with her credentials, arranges for Jane to take up the post of governess at Thornfield in two weeks.

As Jane prepares to leave for Thornfield, Bessie comes to visit. She brings her son—she has married a coachman named Robert Leaven—and fills Jane in on the news from the Reeds' home; she admires Jane's educational and artistic progress. Bessie also informs Jane that a relative of Jane's—a Mr. Eyre—came to Mrs. Reed hoping to see Jane and disappointed to find her at a school far away as he was about to leave for Madeira.

Chapter XI

Jane travels to Millcote and thence to Thornfield, and Mrs. Fairfax, who turns out to be kind and hospitable, expresses gladness at Jane's arrival. Jane learns that Thornfield belongs to Mr. Rochester, to whom Mrs. Fairfax's husband was related on Mr. Rochester's mother's side, and that Mrs. Fairfax is the housekeeper. Jane meets Adèle Varens, who is Mr. Rochester's ward and is to be Jane's pupil—she is glad that Jane can speak French as well as Mr. Rochester can. She tells Jane that her mother died, and that she later came to live with Mr. Rochester along with her nurse, Sophie. Adèle demonstrates some of her accomplishments for Jane, singing a song and reciting a poem. Jane finds the library, which she is to use as a schoolroom, to be amply equipped for her purposes and begins her work with Adèle. From Mrs. Fairfax, Jane learns that Mr. Rochester's visits are sudden and sporadic and that while Mr. Rochester is sometimes hard to read, he is generally a good employer. Jane also asks if there are ghost stories in the house; Mrs. Fairfax says no, but as she shows Jane the house, they hear a distant laugh. Mrs. Fairfax surmises is the laugh of some servant, perhaps, for instance, of Grace Poole, who helps the housemaid.

Chapter XII

Jane settles in nicely and enjoys the company of Adèle and of Mrs. Fairfax, but still yearns for more from her life. She often walks along corridor of the quiet and isolated third floor of Thornfield Hall, occasionally hearing a laugh, murmur, or other sound that she attributes to Grace Poole. Jane tries to get to know Grace Poole, but finds it difficult to sustain a conversation with her. One afternoon in January, Mrs. Fairfax suggests a day off for Adèle, and Jane sets off to Hay to post a letter for Mrs. Fairfax. On her way, she encounters a dog, which reminds her of a spirit and which leads her to a man and a horse who have slipped on ice. Jane offers to find help, but the man refuses. Jane tells him that Mr. Rochester is the owner of Thornfield Hall and that he is not there at the moment, and that she works as a governess at Thornfield. Jane helps the man onto his horse and, still thinking about the encounter, she posts Mrs. Fairfax's letter and returns to Thornfield. At Thornfield, Jane sees the same dog she saw earlier in the day and realizes that the man she spoke to is Mr. Rochester.

Chapter XIII

Adèle is excited to have Mr. Rochester back, and Jane likes the atmosphere of Thornfield Hall with Mr. Rochester at home. Jane and Adèle are invited to have tea with Mr. Rochester—Jane dresses well for the event, at Mrs. Fairfax's instruction—and Mr. Rochester remarks on the improvements in Adèle since he last saw her. Mr. Rochester then asks Jane questions about her life before her arrival at Thornfield, including her piano playing and her paintings. After Mr. Rochester wishes them all good-night, Jane remarks to Mrs. Fairfax that Mr. Rochester seems "changeful and abrupt" and Mrs. Fairfax says that he has family troubles: Mr.

Rochester's older brother is dead, and before his death, he and Mr. Rochester's father compelled Mr. Rochester into "what he considered a painful position, for the sake of making his fortune" and that Mr. Rochester's "spirit could not brook what he had to suffer in it." Mr. Rochester has distanced himself from his family and now is at Thornfield for less than two weeks at a time.

Chapter XIV

When a box of gifts for Adèle arrives, Mr. Rochester sends her and Mrs. Fairfax off and asks Jane to sit with him. He asks Jane if Jane thinks that he is handsome, and Jane answers, "No, sir." before she can stop herself. She asks him if he is a philanthropist and he says that he is not, but that his conscience and once-tender heart have hardened due to events in his life; he asks Jane if he has any hope of softening again. As Jane ponders his question, he tells Jane that, though she is no more pretty than he is handsome, her "puzzled air becomes" her. He thinks that Jane will be good company to talk to, and he would like to get to know her better. The conversation proceeds somewhat awkwardly, but Mr. Rochester is clearly intrigued by Jane. He's impressed with her honesty, and also sees in her an unadulterated goodness that he feels that he, too, once possessed and that he misses in himself. Jane tries to go put Adèle to bed, but Adèle is off trying on her new dress, and she soons return wearing it—reminding Mr. Rochester, he says, of Adèle's mother.

Chapter XV

Mr. Rochester tells Jane about his relationship with Adèle's mother, an opera-dancer from France named Céline Varens, whom he loved but who cheated on him. Mr. Rochester discovered the betrayal and ended the relationship. Céline Varens had previously claimed that Adèle is Mr. Rochester's daughter. Not positive that he is Adèle's father, Mr. Rochester nonetheless brings her into his household to raise. Jane finds that this makes her even more sympathetic to Adèle than she was before, as Adèle does not have many people to turn to and, thus, looks to Jane for friendship. Jane also gains a feeling of comfort with Mr. Rochester as she gets to know him, though she knows that his kind treatment of her is balanced by the "unjust severity to many others," and thinks that his moodiness stems from his past.

Thinking about Mr. Rochester, Jane finds it difficult to sleep, when a sound startles her. She thinks the noise might be Pilot, Mr. Rochester's dog, but then she hears more—moaning, gurgling, laughing. She receives no response when she calls out. As Jane goes out to find Mrs. Fairfax, she sees smoke in the air and smells burning. She rushes to wake up Mr. Rochester, and finds that his sheets are on fire—she douses the bed with water, extinguishing the flames. He is grateful, but admonishes her not to wake anybody or to tell anybody about the incident. He asks her about the noises she heard; she describes the laughter, which she now attributes to Grace Poole. Mr. Rochester agrees that Grace Poole was laughing, and dismisses Jane, who finds it both difficult to quit his company and difficult to sleep when she does.

Chapter XVI

The next morning, various members of Mr. Rochester's household staff discuss the incident from the night before. Jane engages Grace Poole in an odd conversation about the incident, and wonders if Mr. Rochester really thinks that Grace Poole is responsible for the fire and why he keeps this fact a secret—what possible hold could Grace Poole have over Mr. Rochester? She also finds herself feeling a strange attraction to the man, and wondering if he is interested in her.

That evening, Jane is startled to learn from Mrs. Fairfax that Mr. Rochester has gone to a gathering of "fine, fashionable people" and is expected to be away for at least a week. Mrs. Fairfax tells Jane about Miss Blanche Ingram, whom Mrs. Fairfax encountered at Mr. Rochester's Christmas party. Mr. Rochester and Blanche Ingram sang a duet, and Jane speculates with Mrs. Fairfax about whether Mr. Rochester could possibly be romantically interested in Blanche Ingram. Later, in private, Jane berates herself for possibly thinking that Mr. Rochester could have any interest in Jane, and channels her feelings into creating two portraits—one of herself and one of what she imagines Blanche Ingram to look like.

Thought Questions (students consider while they read)

1. How do Jane's feelings for Mr. Rochester evolve over time?

2. Do you think that Grace Poole is responsible for the fire in Mr. Rochester's room? Why or why not?

3. How does Mr. Rochester's confession about Adèle's mother influence Jane's feelings towards Adèle?

4. How does the typhus fever epidemic change Lowood?

5. What prompts Jane to leave Lowood?

Vocabulary (in order of appearance)

Chapter IX: Spring drew on: she was indeed already come; the frosts of winter had ceased; its snows were melted, its cutting winds ameliorated.

ameliorated:

made something better

Chapter IX: ...we could now endure the play-hour passed in the garden: sometimes on a sunny day it began even to be pleasant and genial, and a greenness grew over those brown beds, which, freshening daily, suggested the thought that Hope traversed them at night, and left each morning brighter traces of her steps.

traversed:

moved, traveled, or extended across or through

Chapter IX: ...it tore asunder the wood, and sent a raving sound through the air, often thickened with wild rain or whirling sleet; and for the forest on its banks, that showed only ranks of skeletons.

asunder:

divided, in or into separate pieces

Chapter IX: April advanced to May: a bright serene May it was; days of blue sky, placid sunshine, and soft western or southern gales filled up its duration.

serene:

calm, peaceful, untroubled, tranquil

placid:

calm, peaceful, with little movement or activity, not easily excited

Chapter IX: That forest-dell, where Lowood lay, was the cradle of fog and fog-bred pestilence...

pestilence:

a virulent or deadly disease that spreads widely and affects many people

Chapter IX: Semi-starvation and neglected colds had predisposed most of the pupils to receive infection: forty-five out of the eighty girls lay ill at one time.

predisposed:

made inclined to or susceptible to

Chapter IX: She was not, I was told, in the hospital portion of the house with the fever patients; for her complaint was consumption, not typhus: and by consumption I, in my ignorance, understood something mild, which time and care would be sure to alleviate.

consumption:

using a resource, or a disease causing the wasting away of the body: tuberculosis

a disease causing the wasting away of the body, tuberculosis

alleviate:

to ease something or make it less severe

Chapter X: I am only bound to invoke Memory where I know her responses will possess some degree of interest...

invoke:

to call on for support or inspiration

Chapter X: I remained an inmate of its walls, after its regeneration, for eight years: six as pupil, and two as teacher; and in both capacities I bear my testimony to its value and importance.

regeneration:

a renewal or restoration to something better

Chapter X: In time I rose to be the first girl of the first class; then I was invested with the office of teacher; which I discharged with zeal for two years...

zeal:

great interest and enthusiasm

Chapter X: ...even then a teacher who occupied the same room with me kept me from the subject to which I longed to recur, by a prolonged effusion of small talk.

effusion:

an unrestrained pouring forth of feelings or words

Chapter X: My ostensible errand on this occasion was to get measured for a pair of shoes...

ostensible:

said to be or appearing to be true, but not necessarily true

Chapter XI: I went up to her, and was received with an affable kiss and shake of the hand.

affable:

easy to talk to, friendly

Chapter XI: The enigma then was explained: this affable and kind little widow was no great dame; but a dependant like myself.

enigma:

a puzzling situation, character, or occurrence

Chapter XI: It was the strain of a forsaken lady, who, after bewailing the perfidy of her lover, calls pride to her aid...

forsaken:

abandoned, deserted

perfidy:

betrayal of faith or trust

Chapter XI: "Is Mr. Rochester an exacting, fastidious sort of man?"

fastidious:

attentive to detail and accuracy, particular or demanding, concerned about cleanliness

Chapter XI: There are people who seem to have no notion of sketching a character, or observing and describing salient points, either in persons or things...

salient:

most notable, important, or significant

Chapter XI: I really did not expect any Grace to answer; for the laugh was as tragic, as preternatural a laugh as any I ever heard; and, but that it was high noon, and that no circumstance of ghostliness accompanied the curious cachinnation...

cachinnation:

loud laughter

Chapter XII: The promise of a smooth career, which my first calm introduction to Thornfield Hall seemed to

pledge, was not belied on a longer acquaintance with the place and its inmates.

belied:

shown to be false

Chapter XII: One afternoon in January, Mrs. Fairfax had begged a holiday for Adèle, because she had a cold; and, as Adèle seconded the request with an ardour that reminded me how precious occasional holidays had been to me in my own childhood, I accorded it, deeming that I did well in showing pliability on the point.

ardour:

enthusiasm, intensity of feeling

pliability:

flexibility, cababality of change, ease in being shaped

Chapter XII: I was in the mood for being useful, or at least officious, I think, for I now drew near him again.

officious:

enthusiastically helpful in an intrusive or domineering way

Chapter XII: I had a theoretical reverence and homage for beauty, elegance, gallantry, fascination...

theoretical:

concerned with general principles or possibilities rather than practical applications or experience

reverence:

deep respect

homage:

tribute or respect paid

gallantry:

courageous behavior, courteous attention

Chapter XIII: Adèle and I had now to vacate the library: it would be in daily requisition as a reception-room for callers.

vacate:

to leave a place or position

requisition:

request for use of something

Chapter XIII: Besides, the eccentricity of the proceeding was piquant: I felt interested to see how he would go on.

eccentricity:

something unusual

piquant:

pleasantly exciting

Chapter XIII: The answer was evasive.

evasive:

seeking to avoid something

Chapter XIV: You would, perhaps, think me rude if I inquired in return whether you are a philanthropist?

philanthropist:

a person seeking to help others through work or donations

Chapter XIV: All right then; limpid, salubrious...

limpid:

clear, transparent

salubrious:

favorable to health or well-being

Chapter XV: After this digression he proceeded—

digression:

shift away from a topic of conversation

Chapter XV: He was proud, sardonic, harsh to inferiority of every description: in my secret soul I knew that his great kindness to me was balanced by unjust severity to many others.

sardonic:

disrespectfully or skeptically humorous

Chapter XV: ...at any rate, I started wide awake on hearing a vague murmur, peculiar and lugubrious, which sounded, I thought, just above me.

lugubrious:

gloomy, full of sadness

Chapter XVI: She said "Good morning, Miss," in her usual phlegmatic and brief manner; and taking up another ring and more tape, went on with her sewing.

phlegmatic:

not easily excited to action, calm, composed

Additional Homework

1. Make a list of five predictions of things you think might happen later in the novel.

2. Continue working on your autobiography.

Day 2 - Discussion of Thought Questions

1. How do Jane's feelings for Mr. Rochester evolve over time?

Time:

5 minutes

Discussion:

When Jane first meets Mr. Rochester, before she knows who she is, she is exhilarated because this meeting is a bit of excitement in her life. When he first gets to Thornfield Hall and Jane gets to know him, she at first is finding her feet in his presence, but grows comfortable after she gets to know him. Gradually, she develops feelings of attachment for him. She unhesitatingly saves him from a fire. The romantic nature of these feelings comes to the surface most openly when she speculates about her chances with Mr. Rochester vis-a-vis Blanche Ingram.

2. Do you think that Grace Poole is responsible for the fire in Mr. Rochester's room? Why or why not?

Time:

5 minutes

Discussion:

So far, Grace Poole seems like the most likely person to have set the fire, and, yet, that fact is not definitively confirmed. Students may note that Jane herself seems suspicious and uncertain, and that Mr. Rochester never definitively said that Grace was the arsonist.

3. How does Mr. Rochester's confession about Adèle's mother influence Jane's feelings towards Adèle?

Time:

5 minutes

Discussion:

The fact that Adèle is relatively alone in the world—that her mother is lost and that, even if Mr. Rochester is Adèle's father, he does not publicly recognize Adèle as his daughter—makes Jane, who also feels alone in the world, feel closer to the girl. Jane empathizes with Adèle, and also realizes that Adèle appreciate's Jane's influence and friendship as a governess in a way that other students might not.

4. How does the typhus fever epidemic change Lowood?

Time:

5 minutes

Discussion:

The typhus fever epidemic, during which many students die but many other students are given greater freedom, raises public awareness of the dire conditions under which Lowood students live, and an inquiry is made. Conditions improve, and Mr. Brocklehurst's tasks are supervised closely, as is the general management of the school. However, Jane loses her friend Helen, and Miss Temple and other compassionate teachers and students clearly struggle during this time.

5. What prompts Jane to leave Lowood?

Time:

5 minutes

Discussion:

Miss Temple has been Jane's mentor throughout Jane's stay at Lowood, first as Jane's teacher and then as her colleague. When Miss Temple gets married and leaves the school, Jane feels at first disoriented and without grounding. Gradually, this lack of groundedness shifts into a sense of possibility—an idea that could be more out there outside of the boundaries of Lowood. Jane begins to feel a new lust for adventure and change, and wants to learn more about the world.

Day 2 - Short Answer Evaluation

1. What inspires Jane to leave Lowood?

   _____

2. When Helen Burns is sick and Jane is unable to go see her, with whom does Jane spend much of her time?

   _____

3. Who writes to Jane telling her of a position available at Thornfield?

   _____

4. Where does Mr. Rochester go the day after the fire at Thornfield?

   _____

5. With whom did Mr. Rochester once sing a duet?

   _____

6. What is the name of Mr. Rochester's dog?

   _____

7. Jane creates two portraits while wrestling with her feelings for Mr. Rochester. Whom do these portraits portray?

   _____

8. What job does Mrs. Fairfax have in Mr. Rochester's household?

   _____

9. How is Mrs. Fairfax related to Mr. Rochester?

_____

10. Who is Adèle's mother?

_____

Answer Key

1. Miss Temple leaves to get married and Jane leaves soon after Miss Temple's departure.
2. Jane spends much of her time with Mary Ann Wilson, another Lowood student.
3. Mrs. Fairfax writes to Jane.
4. Mr. Rochester goes to a gathering at the Leas, home of Mr. Eshton.
5. He once sang a duet with Blanche Ingram.
6. Mr. Rochester's dog's name is Pilot.
7. She creates one portrait of herself and one portrait of what she thinks Blanche Ingram might look like.
8. Mrs. Fairfax is Mr. Rochester's housekeeper.
9. She is related to him by marriage through her late husband, on Mr. Rochester's mother's side of the family.
10. Adèle's mother is Céline Varens.

Day 2 - Crossword Puzzle

ACROSS

3. Loud laughter
5. Courageous behavior, courteous attention
7. Easy to talk to, friendly
9. Betrayal of faith or trust
10. Enthusiastically helpful in an intrusive or domineering way
14. Clear, transparent
15. Favorable to health or well-being
16. Mrs _____ answers Jane€™s advertisement
18. Mr _____ is made to change the way Lowood is run

19. Deep respect
20. Gloomy, full of sadness

DOWN

1. Most notable, important, or significant
2. Not easily excited to action, calm, composed
4. Shown to be false
6. Request for use of something
8. A puzzling situation, character, or occurrence
11. Abandoned, deserted
12. Shift away from a topic of conversation
13. Seeking to avoid something
17. Jane has a friend named Helen _____

Crossword Puzzle Answer Key

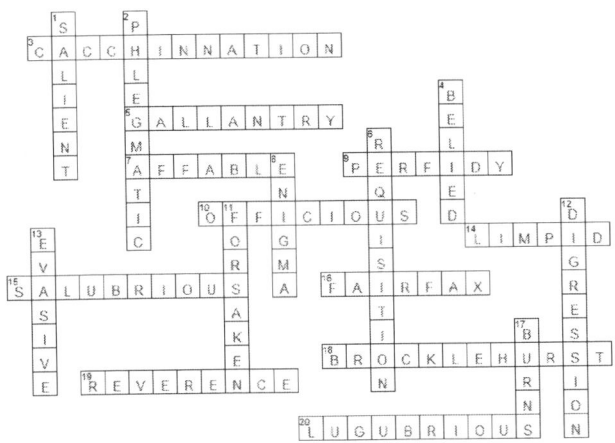

ACROSS

3. Loud laughter
5. Courageous behavior, courteous attention
7. Easy to talk to, friendly
9. Betrayal of faith or trust
10. Enthusiastically helpful in an intrusive or domineering way
14. Clear, transparent
15. Favorable to health or well-being
16. Mrs. _____ answers Jane's advertisement.
18. Mr. _____ is made to change the way Lowood is run.

19. Deep respect
20. Gloomy, full of sadness

DOWN

1. Most notable, important, or significant
2. Not easily excited to action, calm, composed
4. Shown to be false
6. Request for use of something
8. A puzzling situation, character, or occurrence
11. Abandoned, deserted
12. Shift away from a topic of conversation
13. Seeking to avoid something
17. Jane has a friend named Helen _____.

Day 2 - Vocabulary Quiz

Terms

1. _____ asunder
2. _____ traversed
3. _____ alleviate
4. _____ invoke
5. _____ zeal
6. _____ affable
7. _____ enigma
8. _____ perfidy
9. _____ reverence
10. _____ vacate
11. _____ gallantry
12. _____ evasive
13. _____ limpid
14. _____ lugubrious
15. _____ theoretical
16. _____ belied
17. _____ fastidious
18. _____ regeneration
19. _____ forsaken
20. _____ salient

Answers

A. betrayal of faith or trust
B. to ease something or make it less severe
C. courageous behavior, courteous attention
D. to call on for support or inspiration
E. a renewal or restoration to something better
F. to leave a place or position
G. moved, traveled, or extended across or through
H. most notable, important, or significant
I. seeking to avoid something
J. clear, transparent
K. deep respect
L. abandoned, deserted
M. concerned with general principles or possibilities rather than practical applications or experience
N. gloomy, full of sadness
O. great interest and enthusiasm
P. easy to talk to, friendly
Q. a puzzling situation, character, or occurrence
R. shown to be false
S. divided, in or into separate pieces
T. attentive to detail and accuracy, particular or demanding, concerned about cleanliness

Answer Key

1. S asunder: divided, in or into separate pieces
2. G traversed: moved, traveled, or extended across or through
3. B alleviate: to ease something or make it less severe
4. D invoke: to call on for support or inspiration
5. O zeal: great interest and enthusiasm
6. P affable: easy to talk to, friendly
7. Q enigma: a puzzling situation, character, or occurrence
8. A perfidy: betrayal of faith or trust
9. K reverence: deep respect
10. F vacate: to leave a place or position
11. C gallantry: courageous behavior, courteous attention
12. I evasive: seeking to avoid something
13. J limpid: clear, transparent
14. N lugubrious: gloomy, full of sadness
15. M theoretical: concerned with general principles or possibilities rather than practical applications or experience
16. R belied: shown to be false
17. T fastidious: attentive to detail and accuracy, particular or demanding, concerned about cleanliness
18. E regeneration: a renewal or restoration to something better
19. L forsaken: abandoned, deserted
20. H salient: most notable, important, or significant

Day 2 - Classroom Activities

1. Design Your Own School

Kind of Activity:

Mixed Media

Objective:

Students will consider what they think education should look like.

Common Core Standards:

CCSS.ELA-LITERACY.RL.11-12.2; CCSS.ELA-Literacy.SL.11-12.1; CCSS.ELA-Literacy.SL.11-12.4; CCSS.ELA-Literacy.SL.11-12.5

Time:

45 minutes

Structure:

1. As a class, students should discuss what they think is good and bad about Jane's educational experience at Lowood. Make a collective list of these pros and cons. How do the student's ideas of Lowood link to their ideas of education today? Should they look at their own school and Lowood in the same way?

2. In groups, students should should design their own schools based on their own views of what education should look like. In their school design projects, they should include:

a. a description and visual representation of the school building and facilities

b. a mission statement for the school describing its educational philosophy and goals

c. a list of classes available with descriptions for each class

d. anything else they think a school should have (e.g. extracurriculars, students support.)

Students can use whatever materials are at hand to create their designs for their schools. These can include, but are not limited to:

-art supplies

-PowerPoint

-computer drawing tools

-digital cameras

After completing their projects, students should present their designs to each other.

Ideas for Differentiated Instruction:

Use mixed-level groupings for these projects.

Provide models of the different sections of the project for students who struggle.

Assessment Ideas:

Students' school designs can be graded for:

-completion

-effort and creativity

-grammar and mechanics

2. Education Discussion

Kind of Activity:

Group Discussion

Objective:

Students will consider the things they are learning in school and how they will help them later.

Common Core Standards:

CCSS.ELA-LITERACY.RL.11-12.2; CCSS.ELA-Literacy.SL.11-12.1

Time:

15 minutes

Structure:

Discuss Jane's experiences at Lowood. What was Jane learning? How did her knowledge from school contribute to the plans she made for her future, and to her experiences at Thornfield so far?

Students should be encouraged, then, to make connections between Jane's education and their own. In pairs, students should consider and discuss the following questions:

1. What are your favorite subjects in school? Why?

2. What are your least favorite subjects in school? Why?

3. What do you think are the most useful subjects in school? Why?

4. What things are you learning now that you think will be useful to you later in life? How?

This activity can be done again from the points of view of various characters in *Jane Eyre*.

Ideas for Differentiated Instruction:

Encourage students to delve deep into these discussions; provide a list of suggested follow-up questions (for example, "How would you use that knowledge?" or "Is the problem the teacher, or the content?") if students are uncertain how to pursue a topic.

Assessment Ideas:

This activity can function as an informal assessment of students' thoughts about ideas in the novel. If students do later answer the same questions from the points of view of characters from the novel, they can set up a table-style chart, create a Venn Diagram, or write a short essay comparing their answers with the imagined answers from the point of view of one of the characters in the novel.

Day 3 - Reading Assignment, Questions, Vocabulary

Read *Jane Eyre,* Chapters XVII-XXIV. (These chapters can be split up as needed between reading in class and reading at home.)

Common Core Objectives

- CCSS.ELA-Literacy.RL.11-12.3
  Analyze the impact of the author's choices regarding how to develop and relate elements of a story or drama (e.g., where a story is set, how the action is ordered, how the characters are introduced and developed).

- CCSS.ELA-Literacy.RL.11-12.5
  Analyze how an author's choices concerning how to structure specific parts of a text (e.g., the choice of where to begin or end a story, the choice to provide a comedic or tragic resolution) contribute to its overall structure and meaning as well as its aesthetic impact.

- CCSS.ELA-Literacy.W.11-12.3
  Write narratives to develop real or imagined experiences or events using effective technique, well-chosen details, and well-structured event sequences.

- CCSS.ELA-Literacy.W.11-12.6
  Use technology, including the Internet, to produce, publish, and update individual or shared writing products in response to ongoing feedback, including new arguments or information.

- CCSS.ELA-Literacy.SL.11-12.1
  Initiate and participate effectively in a range of collaborative discussions (one-on-one, in groups, and teacher-led) with diverse partners on grades 11-12 topics, texts, and issues, building on others' ideas and expressing their own clearly and persuasively.

Note that it is perfectly fine to expand any day's work into two days depending on the characteristics of the class, particularly if the class will engage in all of the suggested classroom exercises and activities and discuss all of the thought questions.

Content Summary for Teachers

Chapter XVII

After ten days, Mr. Rochester has not returned, and Jane deals with her disappointment by focusing on her professional role. A few weeks later, Mrs. Fairfax receives a letter from Mr. Rochester announcing that he will return in three days and will bring guests with him. Jane hears more about Grace Poole, learning that Grace Poole earns a large salary, is saving her money, and has a role within the household that she understands well and that not everyone could do. Jane feels there is something mysterious in the household that she does not understand.

Mr. Rochester arrives with Miss Ingram and various others. Jane keeps an impatient Adèle content and entertained, and Jane and Mrs. Fairfax discuss Mr. Rochester's interactions with Miss Ingram. Mrs. Fairfax tells Jane that, after Mrs. Fairfax remarked to Mr. Rochester that Adèle wanted very much to meet the visiting ladies, Mr. Rochester requested that Adèle and Jane join the him that evening. That evening, Jane and Adèle make their appearance; Adèle introduces herself to the ladies and they shower her with attention. Jane finds herself observing Mr. Rochester, who is focused on his guests, and suddenly sees him as extremely attractive.

The guests discuss with Adèle with Mr. Rochester, leading to a discussion of governesses, in general, and Jane, in particular. Blanche Ingram states that she wants a husband who is devoted to her rather than to his own reflection in the mirror. She enlists Mr. Rochester to sing a song as she accompanies him on the piano. Jane tries to slip away, but finds herself rivited by Mr. Rochester's singing voice. Mr. Rochester asks her to stay, then, noticing that she is sad, lets her leave, but tells her that he wishes her to spend time with the guests every evening that they are there. He then says, "Good-night, my —" cutting himself off abruptly before finishing the statement.

Chapter XVIII

One evening, the Mr. Rochester and his visitors decide to play charades. Mr. Rochester selects several ladies, including Miss Ingram, to be part of his group; he invites Jane, but she decides not to play, leading Lady Ingram to insult her. Jane watches the game and, in particular, watches the interactions between Mr. Rochester and Miss Ingram. Jane notices that, while Miss Ingram has many impressive qualities and attainments, these hide an inner hollowness and lack of empathy, as evidenced by Miss Ingram's disdainful treatment of Adèle. Jane notes Mr. Rochester, too, observing Miss Ingram's positive and negative attributes. Miss Ingram has not managed to charm Mr. Rochester, and if he marries Miss Ingram, Jane concludes, it would not be out of all-consuming love.

On another evening, after Mr. Rochester has been away for the day, Adèle announces his return. The man who arrives is not, in fact, Mr. Rochester, but a man of a similar age—Mr. Mason—who speaks of Mr. Rochester as if they are friends. Jane infers that he has come from the West Indies. It surprises Jane to think that Mr. Rochester ever travelled there. A fortune-teller knocks; at first the party is inclined to turn her away or even have her arrested, but she is invited in. She states that she will only tell the fortunes of young and single women. She at tells first Blanche Ingram's fortune and then the fortunes of Mary Ingram and Amy and Louisa Eshton all at once. She refuses to leave before she has also told the fortune of the one other young and single woman there: Jane.

Chapter XIX

Jane consults the fortune-teller, who states that Jane feels alone but is within reach of happiness—and then reveals herself to be Mr. Rochester in disguise. Jane tells Mr. Rochester of the arrival of Mr. Mason and Mr. Rochester is alarmed. He asks Jane to take a look to check on his guests' interactions with Mr. Mason. She reports back that Mr. Mason is talking and laughing with Mr. Rochester's guests. Mr. Rochester asks Jane what she would do if all of the guests turned on him or told Jane not to associate with him, and Jane responds that she would stand by him. Ultimately, Mr. Rochester shows Mr. Mason to a room where he can stay.

Chapter XX

During the night, Jane hears a shrill cry, a struggle, and the sound of someone calling out for help. After calming the guests, Mr. Rochester brings Jane to a tapestry-draped room she saw when Mrs. Fairfax gave her a tour of the house; the tapestry is now pulled back to reveal a door, and Jane hears snarling, laughter, and Grace Poole's voice behind it. In bed in the room is Mr. Mason, who is severely injured. Mr. Rochester instructs Jane to take care of him, but that they not talk to each other. Jane obeys, and then Mr. Rochester returns with a surgeon to care for Mr. Mason's wounds, which seem to include being bitten by a woman—the three men discuss the injuries, and continue to allude to the woman who caused them. Mr. Rochester sends Mr. Mason to stay at the surgeon's house; Mr. Mason asks that Mr. Rochester continue to care for the mysterious woman in question. Jane assumes it is Grace Pool. She and Mr. Rochester talk, somewhat cryptically; Mr. Rochester confesses that he feels vulnerable to Jane, who would desert him if she thought he were acting unethically. Jane says that if he has been a sinner, he must reform himself, rather than depending on anyone else. He implies that he might marry quite soon. The two talk until morning, when Mr. Rochester tells the guests that Mr. Mason had to depart.

Chapter XXI

Jane remembers an incident from when she was six years old when Bessie dreamt of a child, and then was called away to the deathbed of her little sister. Now, Jane dreams repeatedly of an infant, and soon enough Robert Leaven, Bessie's husband, arrives at Thornfield dressed in mourning. He tells Jane that John Reed has died, and that Mrs. Reed is not feeling well and has asked for Jane to come and see her. Jane informs Mr. Rochester, who is learning of Jane's connection to the Reeds for the first time (although John Reed became a notorious scoundrel), and he gives her ten pounds for the journey. She and Mr. Rochester also discuss Mr. Rochester's upcoming marriage, which Jane assumes will be to Miss Ingram: she promises Mr. Rochester that she will not advertise for a new position as long as he makes sure that she and Adèle are both settled elsewhere before he brings his new wife into the house.

Jane stops in at the lodge at Gateshead to spend some time catching up with Bessie. When she arrives at the Reeds' house, Jane also sees Eliza and Georgiana, who are formal but not very welcoming towards Jane. When she speaks to Mrs. Reed, who seems to have some dementia, Mrs. Reed describes why she so disliked Jane and the family's current money troubles, which result from John's constant gambling. She seems to think John is still alive. More than ten days go by before Jane speaks with Mrs. Reed again. In the meantime, Eliza and Georgiana gradually warm to Jane after Jane shows them her drawings (including one of Mr. Rochester) and agrees to sketch their portraits, and it comes out that Eliza plans to leave her life behind after Mrs. Reed dies and find a safe place so that she can live as she likes, undisturbed. Georgiana states that this would be consistent with Eliza's previous behavior towards her.

Mrs. Reed tells Jane that she kept from her the news that a relative of Jane's, John Eyre, wished years ago to adopt Jane, bring her to Madeira with him, and bequeath her whatever he had to leave. She kept this news from Jane because she disliked Jane so much. Jane wishes to be reconciled with Mrs. Reed, offering Mrs. Reed her forgiveness, but Mrs. Reed remains firm in her coldness up until the moment of her death.

Chapter XXII

Jane ends up staying at Gateshead for a month. After the funeral, she helps first Georgiana and then Eliza get ready to leave and handle the family business. After leaving Gateshead, Eliza joins a convent in France and Georgiana makes an advantageous marriage. After helping Georgiana and Eliza, Jane returns to Thornfield Hall. She feels a strange joy at returning, and when Mr. Rochester seems thrilled to see her, she realizes the depth of love she has come to feel for him.

Chapter XXIII

About a month later, Mr. Rochester tells Jane that, as he hopes to be married in about a month, he will help Jane find a new job—in fact, he knows of a promising position in Ireland. Jane responds passionately, almost against her will—moving to Ireland would take her far from Thornfield and from Mr. Rochester, and she cannot bear the thought of being separated from him. Hearing this, Mr. Rochester confesses his own love, and says that it is Jane he intends to marry. He is passionately in love with her, and was only teasing about Miss Ingram—she had lost interest of him when he spread a rumor that he had less of a fortune, and he never thought much of her. Jane accepts Mr. Rochester's marriage proposal, and the two walk inside from a rainstorm, kissing, before Jane goes to bed. Overnight, a large tree out front is struck by lightning.

Chapter XXIV

The next morning, Jane is amazed that Mr. Rochester still feels the same way; she is overjoyed, but suspicious of her own happiness. Mrs. Fairfax learns of the engagement; she offers congratulations, but also tells Jane to be careful. Adèle is thrilled with the news and wants to go to Millcote with Mr. Rochester and Jane to look at dresses. They go to a silk warehouse and a jewelry store. Jane does not feel comfortable having Mr. Rochester pick out clothing for her to wear and showering her in jewels, so she wants to write to her uncle in Madeira, hoping that he can somehow help her provide something for Mr. Rochester, as well. Mr. Rochester requests that Jane give up her position as governess, but Jane wishes to continue for the moment, and tries to keep things as much as they were before as possible for the month before the wedding. However, she notes to herself that she is deeply in love, nearly blinded by her passion.

Thought Questions (students consider while they read)

1. Compare Jane with Blanche Ingram.

2. Does Mrs. Reed change over the course of the novel?

3. Are Jane and Mr. Rochester well-matched?

4. Is marrying Mr. Rochester a good choice for Jane?

5. What is Mr. Mason's connection to Mr. Rochester?

Vocabulary (in order of appearance)

Chapter XVII: A joyous stir was now audible in the hall: gentlemen's deep tones and ladies' silvery accents blent harmoniously together, and distinguishable above all, though not loud, was the sonorous voice of the master of

Thornfield Hall, welcoming his fair and gallant guests under its roof.

sonorous:

giving a loud, deep, or resonant sound

Chapter XVII: It was with some trepidation that I perceived the hour approach when I was to repair with my charge to the drawing-room.

trepidation:

a feeling of fear or worry about something that is about to happen

Chapter XVII: I had not intended to love him; the reader knows I had wrought hard to extirpate from my soul the germs of love there detected; and now, at the first renewed view of him, they spontaneously arrived, green and strong!

extirpate:

remove or destroy completely

Chapter XVII: The two proud dowagers, Lady Lynn and Lady Ingram, confabulate together.

confabulate:

have a conversation

Chapter XVII: Oh, gracious, mama! Spare us the enumeration!

enumeration:

listing one by one

Chapter XVII: Amy Eshton, not hearing or not heeding this dictum, joined in with her soft, infantine tone...

heeding:

giving attention to

dictum:

saying or pronouncement

Chapter XVIII: I could not unlove him, because I felt sure he would soon marry this very lady—because I read daily in her a proud security in his intentions respecting her—because I witnessed hourly in him a style of courtship which, if careless and choosing rather to be sought than to seek, was yet, in its very carelessness, captivating, and in its very pride, irresistible.

courtship:

the process of winning someone's favor or affection, the development of a romantic relationship- especially leading to marriage

Chapter XVIII: Too often she betrayed this, by the undue vent she gave to a spiteful antipathy she had conceived against little Adèle: pushing her away with some contumelious epithet if she happened to approach her; sometimes ordering her from the room, and always treating her with coldness and acrimony.

contumelious:

with insulting language or treatment

epithet:

descriptive term, phrase, or nickname applied to a person or thing, often as a term of abuse or contempt

acrimony:

bitterness, hostility, ill feeling

Chapter XVIII: A curious friendship theirs must have been: a pointed illustration, indeed, of the old adage that "extremes meet."

adage:

traditional saying or proverb expressing a common observation

Chapter XVIII: "You see now, my queenly Blanche," began Lady Ingram, "she encroaches. Be advised, my angel girl—and—"

encroaches:

intrudes or advances beyond acceptable limits

Chapter XVIII: My whim is gratified...

whim:

a sudden idea or change of mind

Chapter XIX: A most ingenious quibble!

ingenious:

inventive, clever, original

quibble:

a small objection, a pun, a use of an ambiguity to evade

Chapter XIX: ...it seems to deny, by a mocking glance, the truth of the discoveries I have already made,—to disown the charge both of sensibility and chagrin: its pride and reserve only confirm me in my opinion.

chagrin:

distress at embarrassment or failure

Chapter XX: ...the confusion was inextricable.

inextricable:

incapable of being untangled or solved

Chapter XX: Here, Jane, is an arbour; sit down.

arbour:

a leafy glade or alcove shaded by trees, ivy, shrubs, etc.

Chapter XX: The arbour was an arch in the wall, lined with ivy; it contained a rustic seat.

rustic:

rural, having to do with the countryside

Chapter XX: Again Mr. Rochester propounded his query...

query:

question

Chapter XX: ...you have noticed my tender penchant for Miss Ingram...

penchant:

fondness, strong liking

Chapter XXI: "At all events you will come back: you will not be induced under any pretext to take up a permanent residence with her?"

induced:

convinced or brought about

Chatper XXI: You might have spared yourself the trouble of delivering that tirade...

tirade:

a long and angry speech

Chapter XXII: Then I thought of Eliza and Georgiana; I beheld one the cynosure of a ball-room, the other the inmate of a convent cell; and I dwelt on and analysed their separate peculiarities of person and character.

cynosure:

someone or something that is the center of attraction or attention

Chapter XXII: I had heard from Mrs. Fairfax in the interim of my absence: the party at the hall was dispersed; Mr. Rochester had left for London three weeks ago, but he was then expected to return in a fortnight.

interim:

temporary interval, meantime

Chapter XXII: Mr. Rochester had sometimes read my unspoken thoughts with an acumen to me incomprehensible...

acumen:

sharp insight

Chapter XXIII: "I am no bird; and no net ensnares me; I am a free human being with an independent will, which I now exert to leave you."

ensnares:

catches in a trap

Chapter XXIV: ...and my eyes seemed as if they had beheld the fount of fruition, and borrowed beams from the lustrous ripple.

fount:

a fountain, a source of something valuable

Chapter XXIV: He pursued his theme, however, without noticing my deprecation.

deprecation:

expression of disapproval

Chapter XXIV: Do you really wish the bairn to go?

bairn:

a child

Chapter XXIV: She then peeped round to where I sat; so stern a neighbour was too restrictive to him, in his present fractious mood, she dared whisper no observations, nor ask of him any information.

fractious:

irritable, quarrelsome, unruly

Chapter XXIV: You will stipulate, I see, for peculiar terms—what will they be?

stipulate:

specify a condition or requirement- usually as part of an agreement

Chapter XXIV: ...as he reached me, I asked with asperity, "whom he was going to marry now?"

asperity:

roughness or harshness of tone, condition, or surface

Additional Homework

1. Write a letter from Jane at Thornfield to John Eyre in Madeira. What might she say to him? How do you think she feels about contacting him?

Day 3 - Discussion of Thought Questions

1. Compare Jane with Blanche Ingram.

Time:

5 minutes

Discussion:

Blanche Ingram is lively, beautiful, and accomplished, whereas Jane is more reticent, blending into the background. Blanche is also significantly wealthier than Jane, and accordingly more entitled. However, Jane has depth that Blanche lacks, as well as empathy (especially concerning Adèle).

2. Does Mrs. Reed change over the course of the novel?

Time:

5 minutes

Discussion:

While Mrs. Reed grows ill and is anxious about the financial state of her household, her general values and predilections stay constant. For instance, up until the moment of Mrs. Reed's death, Mrs. Reed refuses to reconcile with Jane, even though Jane is willing to do so. Mrs. Reed's dementia, however, reveals that she struggles with some of the changes in her own life—for example, reconciling herself to John's crimes against the family and his death.

3. Are Jane and Mr. Rochester well-matched?

Time:

5 minutes

Discussion:

On the one hand, Mr. Rochester and Jane have lively and interesting conversations and are clearly drawn to each other. On the other hand, while Jane is open and straightforward, Mr. Rochester plays games with her emotions in order to win her heart. The financial imbalance between the two seems to make Jane uncomfortable, but the two feel very passionately about each other, and both imagine that their love will bring tremendous and positive changes to their lives.

4. Is marrying Mr. Rochester a good choice for Jane?

Time:

10 minutes

Discussion:

Some students may think that Jane should marry Mr. Rochester because she loves him and he loves her. Others may think that Jane should heed Mrs. Fairfax's warning to be careful, and to consider all of the mysterious events that Jane has seen and heard at Thornfield—she has always sensed that there is a mystery within the house, and now seems inclined to ignore all the strange events that once aroused her curiosity.

5. What is Mr. Mason's connection to Mr. Rochester?

Time:

5 minutes

Discussion:

Some students may infer that Mr. Mason has something to do with events from Mr. Rochester's past. Mr. Rochester has referred to having a turbulent past, even to having done terrible things, and his terror at Mr. Mason's arrival may be linked to these events. Students may also believe Mason is connected to whatever it is that Grace Poole does on the third floor, and with all of the mysterious noises and scary events.

Day 3 - Short Answer Evaluation

1. Who is the fortune-teller?

   _____

2. Who performs duets with Mr. Rochester?

   _____

3. What game does Mr. Rochester play with his guests?

   _____

4. What does Eliza do after the death of her mother?

   _____

5. What is the name of Bessie's husband?

   _____

6. Why does Mrs. Reed's family have money troubles?

   _____

7. How does Jane break the ice with Georgiana and Eliza?

   _____

8. How does Mrs. Fairfax react when Jane tells her about the engagement
   between Jane and Mr. Rochester?

   _____

9. How does Mr. Rochester explain the noises his guests hear the night that Mr. Mason is injured?

   _____

10. Why does Mr. Rochester act like he is interested romantically in Miss Ingram?

   _____

Answer Key

1. The fortune-teller turns out to be Mr. Rochester in disguise.
2. Miss Blanche Ingram performs duets with Mr. Rochester.
3. They play charades.
4. Eliza joins a convent after the death of her mother.
5. Bessie's husband's name is Robert Leaven.
6. John, Mrs. Reed's son, gambles away much of the family money before he dies.
7. She offers to sketch their portraits.
8. She congratulates Jane, but also warns Jane to be careful.
9. He tells his guests that a servant has had a nightmare.
10. He pretends to be interested in Miss Ingram in order to make Jane jealous, and make Jane fall in love with him.

Day 3 - Crossword Puzzle

ACROSS
3. Inventive, clever, original
6. A small objection, a pun, a use of an ambiguity to evade
7. Have a conversation
10. Traditional saying or proverb expressing a common observation
12. Giving a loud, deep, or resonant sound
13. Distress at embarrassment or failure
15. "I am no bird; and no net _____ me"
16. Saying or pronouncement
17. Rural, having to do with the countryside
18. Jane often speaks to Adele in _____

DOWN
1. Convinced or brought about
2. The process of winning someone's favor or affection, the development of a romantic relationship- especially leading to marriage
4. A feeling of fear or worry about something that is about to happen
5. Giving attention to
7. With insulting language or treatment
8. Intrudes or advances beyond acceptable limits
9. A child
11. Adele lives in the home of Mr _____.
12. Specify a condition or requirement- usually as part of an agreement
14. Roughness or harshness of tone, condition, or surface

Crossword Puzzle Answer Key

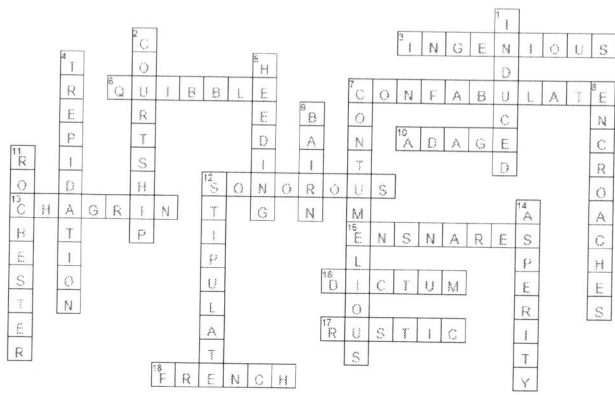

ACROSS

3. Inventive, clever, original
6. A small objection, a pun, a use of an ambiguity to evade
7. Have a conversation
10. Traditional saying or proverb expressing a common observation
12. Giving a loud, deep, or resonant sound
13. Distress at embarrassment or failure
15. "I am no bird; and no net _____ me"
16. Saying or pronouncement
17. Rural, having to do with the countryside
18. Jane often speaks to Adele in _____

DOWN

1. Convinced or brought about
2. The process of winning someone's favor or affection, the development of a romantic relationship- especially leading to marriage
4. A feeling of fear or worry about something that is about to happen
5. Giving attention to
7. With insulting language or treatment
8. Intrudes or advances beyond acceptable limits
9. A child
11. Adele lives in the home of Mr. _____
12. Specify a condition or requirement- usually as part of an agreement
14. Roughness or harshness of tone, condition, or surface

Day 3 - Vocabulary Quiz

Terms

1. _____ trepidation
2. _____ sonorous
3. _____ confabulate
4. _____ extirpate
5. _____ enumeration
6. _____ heeding
7. _____ dictum
8. _____ adage
9. _____ whim
10. _____ courtship
11. _____ ingenious
12. _____ quibble
13. _____ chagrin
14. _____ penchant
15. _____ interim
16. _____ acumen
17. _____ ensnares
18. _____ bairn
19. _____ deprecation
20. _____ stipulate

Answers

A. listing one by one
B. saying or pronouncement
C. distress at embarrassment or failure
D. expression of disapproval
E. have a conversation
F. giving a loud, deep, or resonant sound
G. fondness, strong liking
H. a child
I. temporary interval, meantime
J. traditional saying or proverb expressing a common observation
K. a sudden idea or change of mind
L. a feeling of fear or worry about something that is about to happen
M. giving attention to
N. a small objection, a pun, a use of an ambiguity to evade
O. specify a condition or requirement—usually as part of an agreement
P. remove or destroy completely
Q. catches in a trap
R. sharp insight
S. inventive, clever, original
T. the process of winning someone's favor or affection, the development of a romantic relationship- especially leading to marriage

Answer Key

1. L trepidation: a feeling of fear or worry about something that is about to happen
2. F sonorous: giving a loud, deep, or resonant sound
3. E confabulate: have a conversation
4. P extirpate: remove or destroy completely
5. A enumeration: listing one by one
6. M heeding: giving attention to
7. B dictum: saying or pronouncement
8. J adage: traditional saying or proverb expressing a common observation
9. K whim: a sudden idea or change of mind
10. T courtship: the process of winning someone's favor or affection, the development of a romantic relationship- especially leading to marriage
11. S ingenious: inventive, clever, original
12. N quibble: a small objection, a pun, a use of an ambiguity to evade
13. C chagrin: distress at embarrassment or failure
14. G penchant: fondness, strong liking
15. I interim: temporary interval, meantime
16. R acumen: sharp insight
17. Q ensnares: catches in a trap
18. H bairn: a child
19. D deprecation: expression of disapproval
20. O stipulate: specify a condition or requirement—usually as part of an agreement

Day 3 - Classroom Activities

1. Discussion about Characters

Kind of Activity:

Group Discussion

Objective:

Students will discuss which characters they identify with in the novel so far and why.

Common Core Standards:

CCSS.ELA-LITERACY.RL.11-12.3; CCSS.ELA-Literacy.SL.11-12.1

Time:

15 minutes

Structure:

Make a list of characters that have been introduced thus far in the novel. The class can brainstorm what they remember about them—how do they treat Jane? What is their function in the story thus far? Do you think they will reappear?

In pairs, students should discuss the following questions:

1. Which characters do you identify with so far in the novel? Why?

2. Which characters do you not identify with so far in the novel? Why?

Students should take notes on their conversations. After the discussions in pairs, come back to the full group, where pairs can share their observations on the characters. Why do some students identify with a particular character while others do not? What makes you connect to a character in a work of literature? Do you like characters who Jane dislikes?

Ideas for Differentiated Instruction:

Provide a list of follow-up questions for pair discussions—for example, "How do you think the character would react in [a given situation]?" "What do you have in common with that character?" "What would allow you to identify with that character more?"

Assessment Ideas:

This can function as an informal assessment of students' understanding of and connections to characters in the novel.

2. Building Suspense

Kind of Activity:

Creative Writing

Objective:

Students will look at how suspense is built in Jane Eyre and will write their own suspenseful stories.

Common Core Standards:

CCSS.ELA-LITERACY.RL.11-12.3; CCSS.ELA-Literacy.RL.11-12.5; CCSS.ELA-Literacy.W.11-12.3; CCSS.ELA-Literacy.W.11-12.6

Time:

45 minutes

Structure:

1. When students enter the classroom, they should write down answers to the following:

-What is suspense?

-Describe a situation you have seen, read about, heard of, or experienced that has been suspenseful.

Students should then share their answers with the class.

2. As a class, students should discuss where they have seen moments of suspense in *Jane Eyre* and what makes those moments suspenseful.

3. In pairs, students will examine suspenseful passages from *Jane Eyre*. They should consider the following:

-What questions are raised in this passage?

-What questions are answered?

-What makes this passage suspenseful? How does the author do it?

After discussing the passages in pairs, the students should share out their findings as a class.

4. Students should then write their own suspenseful stories. In their stories, they should:

a. create a situation in which a character has some sort of looming problem, danger, approaching deadline, or exciting thing that is being anticipated

b. drop hints in the story, but leave the reader wanting to know more through the story

c. use details to create a feeling of mystery and/or anticipation

d. include surprising moments or elements

e. resolve the situation

When the stories are complete, students should upload them to a class blog or document-sharing site, such as GoogleDocs, to create a class collection of suspenseful stories.

Ideas for Differentiated Instruction:

Some passages that students can look at to analyze suspense in *Jane Eyre* are:

Chapter XI:

'Mrs. Fairfax stayed behind a moment to fasten the trap-door; I, by drift of groping, found the outlet from the attic, and proceeded to descend the narrow garret staircase. I lingered in the long passage to which this led, separating the front and back rooms of the third storey: narrow, low, and dim, with only one little window at the far end, and looking, with its two rows of small black doors all shut, like a corridor in some Bluebeard's castle.

Day 3 - Classroom Activities

While I paced softly on, the last sound I expected to hear in so still a region, a laugh, struck my ear. It was a curious laugh; distinct, formal, mirthless. I stopped: the sound ceased, only for an instant; it began again, louder: for at first, though distinct, it was very low. It passed off in a clamorous peal that seemed to wake an echo in every lonely chamber; though it originated but in one, and I could have pointed out the door whence the accents issued.

"Mrs. Fairfax!" I called out: for I now heard her descending the great stairs. "Did you hear that loud laugh? Who is it?"

"Some of the servants, very likely," she answered: "perhaps Grace Poole."

"Did you hear it?" I again inquired.

"Yes, plainly: I often hear her: she sews in one of these rooms. Sometimes Leah is with her; they are frequently noisy together."

The laugh was repeated in its low, syllabic tone, and terminated in an odd murmur.

"Grace!" exclaimed Mrs. Fairfax.

I really did not expect any Grace to answer; for the laugh was as tragic, as preternatural a laugh as any I ever heard; and, but that it was high noon, and that no circumstance of ghostliness accompanied the curious cachinnation; but that neither scene nor season favoured fear, I should have been superstitiously afraid. However, the event showed me I was a fool for entertaining a sense even of surprise.

The door nearest me opened, and a servant came out,—a woman of between thirty and forty; a set, square-made figure, red-haired, and with a hard, plain face: any apparition less romantic or less ghostly could scarcely be conceived.

"Too much noise, Grace," said Mrs. Fairfax. "Remember directions!" Grace curtseyed silently and went in.

"She is a person we have to sew and assist Leah in her housemaid's work," continued the widow; "not altogether unobjectionable in some points, but she does well enough. By-the-bye, how have you got on with your new pupil this morning?"

Chapter XV:

'I tried again to sleep; but my heart beat anxiously: my inward tranquillity was broken. The clock, far down in the hall, struck two. Just then it seemed my chamber-door was touched; as if fingers had swept the panels in groping a way along the dark gallery outside. I said, "Who is there?" Nothing answered. I was chilled with fear.

All at once I remembered that it might be Pilot, who, when the kitchen-door chanced to be left open, not unfrequently found his way up to the threshold of Mr. Rochester's chamber: I had seen him lying there myself in the mornings. The idea calmed me somewhat: I lay down. Silence composes the nerves; and as an unbroken hush now reigned again through the whole house, I began to feel the return of slumber. But it was not fated that I should sleep that night. A dream had scarcely approached my ear, when it fled affrighted, scared by a marrow-freezing incident enough.

This was a demoniac laugh—low, suppressed, and deep—uttered, as it seemed, at the very keyhole of my chamber door. The head of my bed was near the door, and I thought at first the goblin-laugher stood at my bedside—or rather, crouched by my pillow: but I rose, looked round, and could see nothing; while, as I still gazed, the unnatural sound was reiterated: and I knew it came from behind the panels. My first impulse was to rise and fasten the bolt; my next, again to cry out, "Who is there?"

Something gurgled and moaned. Ere long, steps retreated up the gallery towards the third-storey staircase: a door had lately been made to shut in that staircase; I heard it open and close, and all was still.

"Was that Grace Poole? and is she possessed with a devil?" thought I. Impossible now to remain longer by myself: I must go to Mrs. Fairfax. I hurried on my frock and a shawl; I withdrew the bolt and opened the door with a trembling hand. There was a candle burning just outside, and on the matting in the gallery. I was surprised at this circumstance: but still more was I amazed to perceive the air quite dim, as if filled with smoke; and, while looking to the right hand and left, to find whence these blue wreaths issued, I became further aware of a strong smell of burning.

Something creaked: it was a door ajar; and that door was Mr. Rochester's, and the smoke rushed in a cloud from thence. I thought no more of Mrs. Fairfax; I thought no more of Grace Poole, or the laugh: in an instant, I was within the chamber. Tongues of flame darted round the bed: the curtains were on fire. In the midst of blaze and vapour, Mr. Rochester lay stretched motionless, in deep sleep.

"Wake! wake!" I cried. I shook him, but he only murmured and turned: the smoke had stupefied him. Not a moment could be lost: the very sheets were kindling, I rushed to his basin and ewer; fortunately, one was wide and the other deep, and both were filled with water. I heaved them up, deluged the bed and its occupant, flew back to my own room, brought my own water-jug, baptized the couch afresh, and, by God's aid, succeeded in extinguishing the flames which were devouring it.

The hiss of the quenched element, the breakage of a pitcher which I flung from my hand when I had emptied it, and, above all, the splash of the shower-bath I had liberally bestowed, roused Mr. Rochester at last. Though it was now dark, I knew he was awake; because I heard him fulminating strange anathemas at finding himself lying in a pool of water.

"Is there a flood?" he cried.

"No, sir," I answered; "but there has been a fire: get up, do; you are quenched now; I will fetch you a candle."

"In the name of all the elves in Christendom, is that Jane Eyre?" he demanded. "What have you done with me, witch, sorceress? Who is in the room besides you? Have you plotted to drown me?"

"I will fetch you a candle, sir; and, in Heaven's name, get up. Somebody has plotted something: you cannot too soon find out who and what it is."

"There! I am up now; but at your peril you fetch a candle yet: wait two minutes till I get into some dry garments, if any dry there be—yes, here is my dressing-gown. Now run!"

I did run; I brought the candle which still remained in the gallery. He took it from my hand, held it up, and surveyed the bed, all blackened and scorched, the sheets drenched, the carpet round swimming in water.

"What is it? and who did it?" he asked. I briefly related to him what had transpired: the strange laugh I had heard in the gallery: the step ascending to the third storey; the smoke,—the smell of fire which had conducted me to his room; in what state I had found matters there, and how I had deluged him with all the water I could lay hands on.'

Assessment Ideas:

Students' stories can be graded for:

-completion

-understanding of suspense

-grammar and mechanics

Day 4 - Reading Assignment, Questions, Vocabulary

Read *Jane Eyre,* Chapters XV-XXXII. (These chapters can be split up as needed between reading in class and reading at home.)

Common Core Objectives

- CCSS.ELA-LITERACY.RL.11-12.2
  Determine two or more themes or central ideas of a text and analyze their development over the course of the text, including how they interact and build on one another to produce a complex account; provide an objective summary of the text.

- CCSS.ELA-LITERACY.RL.11-12.3
  Analyze the impact of the author's choices regarding how to develop and relate elements of a story or drama (e.g., where a story is set, how the action is ordered, how the characters are introduced and developed).

- CCSS.ELA-Literacy.RL.11-12.6
  Analyze a case in which grasping a point of view requires distinguishing what is directly stated in a text from what is really meant (e.g., satire, sarcasm, irony, or understatement).

- CCSS.ELA-Literacy.SL.11-12.1
  Initiate and participate effectively in a range of collaborative discussions (one-on-one, in groups, and teacher-led) with diverse partners on grades 11-12 topics, texts, and issues, building on others' ideas and expressing their own clearly and persuasively.

- CCSS.ELA-Literacy.SL.11-12.3
  Evaluate a speaker's point of view, reasoning, and use of evidence and rhetoric, assessing the stance, premises, links among ideas, word choice, points of emphasis, and tone used.

Note that it is perfectly fine to expand any day's work into two days depending on the characteristics of the class, particularly if the class will engage in all of the suggested classroom exercises and activities and discuss all of the thought questions.

Content Summary for Teachers

Chapter XXV

The wedding day draws closer, and Jane feels anxiety and anticipation about the prospect of becoming Mrs. Rochester. When Mr. Rochester has been away, Jane awaits his arrival impatiently; when he arrives, Jane describes to him dreams she has had, dreams of wandering terrified when separated from Mr. Rochester, and of taking an infant through the ruins of Thornfield. After waking up from these dreams, Jane says, she saw a woman first trying on and then tearing Jane's wedding veil. Mr. Rochester protests that she must have dreamed this as well, but Jane's veil was, in fact, torn. Mr. Rochester comforts her, attributes the tearing of the veil to Grace Poole, and says he will tell Jane why he keeps Grace Poole in his house a year hence. Jane spends the night in Adèle's nursery.

Chapter XXVI

The wedding begins. Mr. Wood, the clergyman, asks if there are any possible impediments that would stand in the way of the marriage proceeding lawfully—and a solicitor named Briggs states that there is an impediment: Mr. Rochester already has a wife. Mr. Mason, he says, can testify to the fact that Mr. Rochester's wife is still alive. Mr. Mason is also present at the wedding; he says that his sister is Mr. Rochester's wife, and that she is living at Thornfield Hall. Mr. Rochester affirms that this is true, and that he married her not knowing that she was "mad," and "came of a mad family." His wife's name is Bertha; her condition deteriorated rapidly after they were married, and she now she lives in the attic at Thornfield.

Everyone at the wedding returns with Mr. Rochester and Jane to Thornfield, and Rochester leads them to the room with the tapestry—the site of Mr. Mason's injury. There Grace Poole supervises a woman who is pacing the room like a wild animal, and who tries to strangle and bite Mr. Rochester. He defends himself, but will not hit her. Mr. Rochester introduces the woman to the assembled people as his wife. He desperately wanted to find, despite his marital status, some happiness in love with Jane. He sends everyone from the room.

As they leave, Mr. Briggs tells Jane that Mr. Mason met Jane's uncle John Eyre in Madeira. Jane's uncle had told Mr. Mason about Jane's upcoming marriage, and Mr. Mason had told Jane's uncle about Mr. Rochester's marital situation. John Eyre, on his sick-bed and therefore unable to travel, sent Mr. Briggs to try to stop the wedding. Mr. Mason now plans to return and reassure Mr. Eyre that the marriage did not take place, but he is concerned that Mr. Eyre might have died already. When the guests leave, Jane shuts herself in her room, desperately grieving the loss of her marriage and her dreams.

Chapter XXVII

The next morning, Rochester is surprised at Jane's lack of affect and begs for her forgiveness. He explains the story of his wife—after Mr. Rochester's father made his elder brother the sole heir of the estate, he determined to find a wealthy wife for Mr. Rochester so that he would not be penniless. His father had worked with Bertha Mason's father, and Mr. Rochester was sent to Jamaica to meet her. He was deeply attracted to her and married her, and would learn only later that her mother and brother were lunatics. (The elder Mr. Rochester had known, but had withheld the information.) Bertha's sanity deteriorated quickly, and she was violent and incapable of communication. Mr. Rochester suffered for years with her in Jamaica, during which time his father and brother died; after becoming so miserable he was nearly suicidal, he returned to Europe with his wife and confined her to the attic at Thornfield in secret, hiring Grace Poole to care for her and a surgeon to tend her, but telling no one else. He traveled Europe, taking lovers rashly and leaving Bertha behind, for years before he fell in love with Jane.Jane forgives Mr. Rochester, but remains devastated, betrayed, and fearful of her love and vulnerability to someone who has proven so dishonest and unstable. Jane decides she cannot stay at Thornfield Hall, a choice that devastates both her and Mr. Rochester. She leaves that very night, and the next morning finds a driver to take her a long distance from Thornfield.

Chapter XXVIII

After two days of travelling, Jane arrives at a place called Whitcross, and spends the night on the moor, thinking of Mr. Rochester. The next day, she finds a small village, where she begins asking around about employment possibilities. There seem to be none. Having no money, she tries to trade her belongings for food, and occasionally even begs for it.

Covered in dirt from her journey and ill from hunger and exhaustion, Jane knocks on the door of the house of two sisters and a brother—Diana, Mary, and St. John Rivers. Jane introduces herself as Jane Elliott and is provided with bread, milk, and a place to sleep. The brother and sisters speculate about Jane's circumstances and leave her to rest.

Chapter XXIX

On Jane's fourth day at the house, she wakes up feeling better and notes that her clothes have been cleaned. She helps Hannah, a servant, pick gooseberries, clearing up misconceptions about her circumstances and also learning more about Diana, Mary, and St. John. Jane tells the Rivers siblings about her personal history, including her teaching experience, but leaves out the details of her recent loss. She asks them to help her become independent as soon as possible, and admits that Jane Elliott is not her real name. The Rivers siblings agree that she can stay with them and that they will support her.

Chapter XXX

Jane settles into an atmosphere of comfortable companionship with Diana and Mary, but feels more of a distance in her interactions with St. John. Despite St. John's religious commitment, he does not seem to have settled into the peace of mind that religions contemplation can bring. A month goes by, and Diana and Mary are soon to leave to take up positions as governesses. St. John offers Jane the position of schoolmistress at a village school for girls that he intends to open and Jane accepts the position. St. John, Diana, and Mary learn via letter that their uncle John has died and left them thirty guineas for the purchase of mourning rings, leaving the rest of his fortune to another relative. Jane leaves for her new school position; Diana and Mary leave for their positions as governesses; St. John and Hannah leave the little house for the parsonage.

Chapter XXXI

After Jane's first day of teaching, St. John drops off a present for Jane from his sisters and asks Jane how she is settling in, and she tells him she is grateful for the position. St. John tells Jane that he plans to be a missionary, and as he begins to explain his goals, Miss Oliver, the young woman who provided Jane's living accommodations, visits to see how Jane is settling in. Miss Oliver invites St. John to come back with her to visit her father, who she says would welcome some company, but St. John declines.

Chapter XXXII

Jane begins to get to know and like her new students. She becomes a welcomed and appreciated member of the community, and Rosamond Oliver often visits her at home and at school—her visits frequently coinciding with St. John's daily catechism lessons. St. John loves Rosamond Oliver, and she returns his feelings, but he will not let himself act on these feelings. One day, at Rosamond Oliver's request, Jane sketches a picture of her. Rosamond's father then invites Jane to Vale Hall, the Oliver family home. He compliments Jane's work at Morton school and praises St. John and the Rivers family, seeming to indicate that he would not be averse to a marriage between St. John and Rosamond Oliver.

In November, St. John comes to visit Jane. He is impressed with Jane's portrait of Rosamond, and Jane tries to convince St. John that he should act his feelings for her. St. John, though, is not convinced that Rosamond Oliver would make a good missionary's wife, even though he feels great affection for her. Jane tells St. John that he does not have to be a missionary, that St. John should consider both Rosamond Oliver's feelings and his own. St. John looks closely at the portrait again as he departs, but also seems to be looking oddly closely at Jane.

Thought Questions (students consider while they read)

1. Even if Mr. Rochester did not have a wife, would he make a good husband for Jane?

2. How do Jane's previous experiences help her survive once she leaves Mr. Rochester's house?

3. What should St. John Rivers do about his feelings for Rosamond Oliver?

4. Do you think that this is the end of the story for Jane and Mr. Rochester? Why or why not?

5. What are some prejudices that characters overcome after Jane leaves Thornfield Hall?

Vocabulary (in order of appearance)

Chapter XXV: ...for not to me appertained that suit of wedding raiment...

appertained:

related to, was appropriate

Chapter XXV: A puerile tear dimmed my eye while I looked—a tear of disappointment and impatience; ashamed of it, I wiped it away.

puerile:

childish, immature

Chapter XXV: I exclaimed, seized with hypochondriac foreboding.

hypochondriac:

excessively preoccupied with or worried about health

foreboding:

feeling that something bad will happen

Chapter XXV: ...joy made me agile...

agile:

lively, able to move or think quickly

Chapter XXV: The shape standing before me had never crossed my eyes within the precincts of Thornfield Hall before...

precinct:

an area within specific or defined boundaries

Chapter XXVI: "Mr. Wood is in the vestry, sir, putting on his surplice."

vestry:

a room or building attached to a church used for meetings, a meeting of parishioners, a group of parishioners holding a meeting

Chapter XXVI: I know not whether the day was fair or foul; in descending the drive, I gazed neither on sky nor earth: my heart was with my eyes; and both seemed migrated into Mr. Rochester's frame.

migrated:

moved from one area to another

Chapter XXVI: "I have a witness to the fact, whose testimony even you, sir, will scarcely controvert."

controvert:

dispute, oppose, or deny the truth of something

Chapter XXVII: "You know I am a scoundrel, Jane?"

scoundrel:

a dishonest or unprincipled person

Chapter XXVII: "Sir, I do not wish to act against you," I said; and my unsteady voice warned me to curtail my sentence.

curtail:

reduce in quantity, make less by cutting off

Chapter XXVII: I have a place to repair to, which will be a secure sanctuary from hateful reminiscences, from unwelcome intrusion—even from falsehood and slander.

sanctuary:

a safe place providing protection

Chapter XXVII: "And did you ever hear that my father was an avaricious, grasping man?"

avaricious:

greedy, having an extreme desire for gaining and hoarding wealth

Chapter XXVII: ...but that is the sort of pity native to callous, selfish hearts...

callous:

being hardened, insensitive, having a disregard for others

Chapter XXVII: your air was often diffident, and altogether that of one refined by nature, but absolutely unused to society, and a good deal afraid of making

herself disadvantageously conspicuous by some solecism or blunder

solecism:

grammatical mistake, error in behavior or good manners

Chapter XXVII: I was experiencing an ordeal...

ordeal:

severe experience or test

Chapter XXVII: ...and I must renounce love and idol.

renounce:

to give up voluntarily

Chapter XXVII: Is it better to drive a fellow-creature to despair than to transgress a mere human law, no man being injured by the breach?

transgress:

to violate or go beyond the boundary of something

Chapter XXVII: Still indomitable was the reply...

indomitable:

impossible to subdue, overcome, or defeat

Chapter XXVII: I could yet spare him the bitter pang of bereavement.

bereavement:

period of grief after loss

Chapter XXVII: Oh, that fear of his self-abandonment—far worse than my abandonment—how it goaded me!

goaded:

provoked or incited

Chapter XXVIII: ...and I, who from man could anticipate only mistrust, rejection, insult, clung to her with filial fondness.

filial:

relating to a son or a daughter

Chapter XXVIII: ...and it is in the unclouded night-sky, where His worlds wheel their silent course, that we read clearest His infinitude, His omnipotence, His omnipresence.

infinitude:

the state of being infinite or without limit

omnipresence:

a state of being in all places at all times

a state of being in all places at all times

Chapter XXVIII:...and it is in the unclouded night-sky, where His worlds wheel their silent course, that we read clearest His infinitude, His omnipotence, His omnipresence.

omnipotence:

a state of having unlimited power

Chapter XXVIII: I walked a long time, and when I thought I had nearly done enough, and might conscientiously yield to the fatigue that almost overpowered me—might relax this forced action, and, sitting down on a stone I saw near, submit resistlessly to the apathy that clogged heart and limb—I heard a bell chime—a church bell.

apathy:

a lack of interest, excitement, or concern

Chapter XXVIII: Oh, for but a crust! for but one mouthful to allay the pang of famine!

allay:

to relieve, lessen, or put at rest

Chapter XXVIII: Entering the gate and passing the shrubs, the silhouette of a house rose to view, black, low, and rather long; but the guiding light shone nowhere.

silhouette:

the general shape and outline of someone or something

Chapter XXIX: "Strange hardships, I imagine—poor, emaciated, pallid wanderer?"

emaciated:

extremely thin due to illness or lack of nutrition

Chapter XXIX: We may, perhaps, succeed in restoring her to them, if she is not obstinate: but I trace lines of force in her face which make me sceptical of her tractability.

obstinate:

stubborn, inflexible

tractability:

easy to manage, deal with, or guide

Chapter XXIX: When she left me, I felt comparatively strong and revived: ere long satiety of repose and desire for action stirred me.

satiety:

a feeling of being full or satisfied

Chapter XXIX: There was no superfluous ornament in the room—not one modern piece of furniture, save a brace of workboxes and a lady's desk in rosewood, which stood on a side-table: everything—including the carpet and curtains—looked at once well worn and well saved.

superfluous:

extra, unnecessary

Chapter XXIX: "I need it, and I seek it so far, sir, that some true philanthropist will put me in the way of getting work which I can do, and the remuneration for which will keep me, if but in the barest necessaries of life."

remuneration:

money paid for work, reward

Chapter XXX: ...he had no more found it, I thought, than had I with my concealed and racking regrets for my broken idol and lost elysium...

elysium:

state of complete happiness, Elysian Fields- place of the blessed after death

Chapter XXXII: ... or would the sight of it bring recollections calculated to enervate and distress?

enervate:

to exhaust, to drain of energy

Additional Homework

1. Write a letter of at least one page giving advice to one of the characters in the novel.

Day 4 - Discussion of Thought Questions

1. Even if Mr. Rochester did not have a wife, would he make a good husband for Jane?

Time:

10 minutes

Discussion:

Some students may feel that Mr. Rochester loves Jane, and that she loves him, too, and that love is the basis of a solid marriage. Others may feel that Mr. Rochester's lack of straightforwardness about his marriage, as well as the machinations he undertakes to win Jane over, indicate an inner deceptiveness that does not mesh with Jane's inherently honest nature. Some may believe that the two complement each other well, but others may think that Rochester has proven himself dishonorable.

2. How do Jane's previous experiences help her survive once she leaves Mr. Rochester's house?

Time:

10 minutes

Discussion:

Students may think that Jane's experiences teaching and learning in a boarding school, as well as her experience as a governess at Thornfield Hall, provide her with both the qualifications to get the job teaching at the Morton school that St. John opens and the experience to draw on in order to do the job well. Also, students may think that Jane's drawing skills, besides being evidence of impressive accomplishment, consistently provide Jane with a way of breaking the ice with people in new and/or uncomfortable social situations.

3. What should St. John Rivers do about his feelings for Rosamond Oliver?

Time:

10 minutes

Discussion:

Some students may think that St. John should pursue his dreams of becoming a missionary—that his personality will ultimately be unhappy with a settled life at Vale Hall and that Rosamond Oliver will find someone else with whom she can have a happy life. Other students may think that St. John is denying happiness to both himself and Rosamond Oliver by dismissing his feelings for her and not asking her to marry him.

4. Do you think that this is the end of the story for Jane and Mr. Rochester? Why or why not?

Time:

5 minutes

Discussion:

Some students may think that Jane has moved on with her life and has gone on to new things. Other students may think that, because Jane still dreams and thinks about Mr. Rochester at times, that she may in some way cross paths with him again. It is possible that both will change very much when they are separated from each other; this could lead them to be more or less compatible if they meet again.

5. What are some prejudices that characters overcome after Jane leaves Thornfield Hall?

Time:

5 minutes

Discussion:

Jane notices that Hannah has already formed a negative opinion of her based on little information, and takes time to clear up Hannah's misconceptions about her. Jane also jumps to her own conclusions about Hannah's opinions and the roots of those opinions. Jane grows to understand and like her students at the school in Morton as she gets to know them and spends time teaching them.

Day 4 - Short Answer Evaluation

1. Where did Mr. Mason meet Jane's uncle?

    _____

2. Why does Mr. Briggs interrupt the wedding of Jane and Mr. Rochester?

    _____

3. What is Grace Poole's job in Mr. Rochester's household?

    _____

4. What is the name of Mr. Rochester's wife?

    _____

5. What is the last name of St. John, Diana, and Mary?

    _____

6. What jobs do Diana and Mary have?

    _____

7. How does St. John feel about Rosamond Oliver?

    _____

8. What job does St. John provide for Jane?

    _____

9. What does Jane tell Diana, Mary, and St. John is her name?

10. What does the uncle of Diana, Mary, and St. John leave them in his will?

Answer Key

1. Mr. Mason met Jane's uncle in Madeira.
2. Mr. Briggs interrupts the wedding to say that Mr. Rochester is already married.
3. Grace Poole takes care of Mr. Rochester's wife.
4. Her name is Bertha Mason.
5. Their last name is Rivers.
6. They both work as governesses.
7. He loves her, but doesn't want to marry her because he wants to go off into the world and be a missionary. This situation causes him inner conflict, despite his assurances to the contrary.
8. She begins teaching in the school St. John opens for girls in Morton.
9. She tells them that her name is Jane Elliott.
10. He leaves them thirty guineas to buy three mourning rings. The rest of his money, he leaves to another relative.

Day 4 - Crossword Puzzle

ACROSS

5. Feeling that something bad will happen
6. Grammatical mistake, error in behavior or good manners

12. Severe experience or test
13. An area within specific or defined boundaries
14. Lively, able to move or think quickly
15. Traditional saying or proverb expressing a common observation
17. Provoked or incited
18. To give up voluntarily
19. Stubborn, inflexible
20. Blanche _____ is a visitor at Mr. Rochester's home.

DOWN

1. Excessively preoccupied with or worried about health
2. Moved from one area to another
3. To exhaust, to drain of energy
4. Childish, immature
7. Greedy; having an extreme desire for gaining and hoarding wealth
8. Relating to a son or a daughter
9. A safe place providing protection
10. Related to, was appropriate
11. Period of grief after loss
16. Blanche has a sister named _____

Crossword Puzzle Answer Key

ACROSS

5. Feeling that something bad will happen
6. Grammatical mistake; error in behavior or good manners

12. Severe experience or test
13. An area within specific or defined boundaries
14. Lively, able to move or think quickly
15. Traditional saying or proverb expressing a common observation
17. Provoked or incited
18. To give up voluntarily
19. Stubborn, inflexible
20. Blanche _____ is a visitor at Mr. Rochester's home.

DOWN

1. Excessively preoccupied with or worried about health
2. Moved from one area to another
3. To exhaust; to drain of energy
4. Childish, immature
7. Greedy, having an extreme desire for gaining and hoarding wealth
8. Relating to a son or a daughter
9. A safe place providing protection
10. Related to; was appropriate
11. Period of grief after loss
16. Blanche has a sister named _____

Day 4 - Vocabulary Quiz

Terms

1. _____ appertained
2. _____ foreboding
3. _____ puerile
4. _____ sanctuary
5. _____ callous
6. _____ ordeal
7. _____ renounce
8. _____ transgress
9. _____ infinitude
10. _____ emaciated
11. _____ superfluous
12. _____ enervate
13. _____ obstinate
14. _____ apathy
15. _____ bereavement
16. _____ avaricious
17. _____ migrated
18. _____ scoundrel
19. _____ curtail
20. _____ filial

Answers

A. extra, unnecessary
B. relating to a son or a daughter
C. feeling that something bad will happen
D. a lack of interest, excitement, or concern
E. to exhaust, to drain of energy
F. to violate or go beyond the boundary of something
G. moved from one area to another
H. the state of being infinite or without limit
I. being hardened, insensitive, having a disregard for others
J. extremely thin due to illness or lack of nutrition
K. severe experience or test
L. a dishonest or unprincipled person
M. to give up voluntarily
N. greedy, having an extreme desire for gaining and hoarding wealth
O. period of grief after loss
P. reduce in quantity, make less by cutting off
Q. a safe place providing protection
R. stubborn, inflexible
S. childish, immature
T. related to, was appropriate

Answer Key

1. T appertained: related to, was appropriate
2. C foreboding: feeling that something bad will happen
3. S puerile: childish, immature
4. Q sanctuary: a safe place providing protection
5. I callous: being hardened, insensitive, having a disregard for others
6. K ordeal: severe experience or test
7. M renounce: to give up voluntarily
8. F transgress: to violate or go beyond the boundary of something
9. H infinitude: the state of being infinite or without limit
10. J emaciated: extremely thin due to illness or lack of nutrition
11. A superfluous: extra, unnecessary
12. E enervate: to exhaust, to drain of energy
13. R obstinate: stubborn, inflexible
14. D apathy: a lack of interest, excitement, or concern
15. O bereavement: period of grief after loss
16. N avaricious: greedy, having an extreme desire for gaining and hoarding wealth
17. G migrated: moved from one area to another
18. L scoundrel: a dishonest or unprincipled person
19. P curtail: reduce in quantity, make less by cutting off
20. B filial: relating to a son or a daughter

Day 4 - Classroom Activities

1. Teacher-In-Role

Kind of Activity:

Role Play

Objective:

Students will take on the roles of helpful advisers to help Jane make decisions.

Common Core Standards:

CCSS.ELA-LITERACY.RL.11-12.2; CCSS.ELA-Literacy.RL.11-12.6; CCSS.ELA-Literacy.SL.11-12.1; CCSS.ELA-Literacy.SL.11-12.3

Time:

20 minutes

Structure:

1. The teacher should come in either dressed as one of the characters from *Jane Eyre* or wearing a sign with that character's name on it. The teacher should then, in the role of that character, explain to the class the problems that the character faces and then should ask the students for advice.

2. The students should then give the teacher, as if the teacher were the character, advice on the character's situation.

3. Make this activity into a dialogue—don't simply take the students' advice, but challenge it, reminaing in character, pointing out details from the text that might counteract the students' suggestions.

4. Afterwards, either take the role of a different character, or offer students the opportunity to take on different roles themselves, guiding the conversation to ensure that students remain focused on dilemmas in the text.

Ideas for Differentiated Instruction:

The activity could be done online. The teacher could post, as a character, a question that students could answer about that character's dilemma(s).

Assessment Ideas:

This activity can be used informally to assess students' understanding of the characters and events in *Jane Eyre*.

2. Weather Imagery in Jane Eyre

Kind of Activity:

Mixed Media

Objective:

Students will respond to weather imagery, find weather imagery quotations of their own, and draw inferences about these quotations' use in the novel.

Common Core Standards:

CCSS.ELA-LITERACY.RL.11-12.3

Time:

30 minutes

Structure:

1. The teacher should post around the room on chart paper several excerpts from *Jane Eyre* that include descriptions of the weather. The students should walk around and, using markers, responses to or comments about the quotations. What is evocative about these descriptions? Why might Brontë have chosen this particular kind of weather for this particular scene?

2. After giving students a chance to respond to the quotations and to walk around and read each other's responses, the teacher should reconvene the class to discuss all of the quotations. Ask the students:

1. What was your reaction to the quotation?

2. What did it make you think of?

3. Why do you think this description of weather is included?

4. Do you think this description reflects, corresponds to, or contrasts with anything going on in the novel?

3. In pairs, students should then look through the novel and find three other weather descriptions in the novel and write them down.

4. For each weather description chosen, students should draw a picture of what is being described and explain what purpose this weather description might be serving in Jane's story.

Ideas for Differentiated Instruction:

Here are some possible quotations the teacher can post and/or point students towards:

Chapter I:

"There was no possibility of taking a walk that day. We had been wandering, indeed, in the leafless shrubbery an hour in the morning; but since dinner (Mrs. Reed, when there was no company, dined early) the cold winter wind had brought with it clouds so sombre, and a rain so penetrating, that further out-door exercise was now out of the question.

I was glad of it: I never liked long walks, especially on chilly afternoons: dreadful to me was the coming home in the raw twilight, with nipped fingers and toes, and a heart saddened by the chidings of Bessie, the nurse, and humbled by the consciousness of my physical inferiority to Eliza, John, and Georgiana Reed."

Chapter IV:

"I opened the glass-door in the breakfast-room: the shrubbery was quite still: the black frost reigned, unbroken by sun or breeze, through the grounds. I covered my head and arms with the skirt of my frock, and went out to walk in a part of the plantation which was quite sequestrated; but I found no pleasure in the silent trees, the falling fir-cones, the congealed relics of autumn, russet leaves, swept by past winds in heaps, and now stiffened together. I leaned against a gate, and looked into an empty field where no sheep were feeding, where the short grass was nipped and blanched. It was a very grey day; a most opaque sky, 'onding on snaw,' canopied all; thence flakes felt it intervals, which settled on the hard path and on the hoary lea without melting. I stood, a wretched child enough, whispering to myself over and over again, 'What shall I do?—what shall I do?'"

Chapter V:

"The moon was set, and it was very dark; Bessie carried a lantern, whose light glanced on wet steps and gravel road sodden by a recent thaw. Raw and chill was the winter morning: my teeth chattered as I hastened down the drive. There was a light in the porter's lodge: when we reached it, we found the porter's wife just kindling her fire: my trunk, which had been carried down the evening before, stood corded at the door. It wanted but a few minutes of six, and shortly after that hour had struck, the distant roll of wheels announced the coming coach; I went to the door and watched its lamps approach rapidly through the gloom."

Chapter V:

The night passed rapidly. I was too tired even to dream; I only once awoke to hear the wind rave in furious gusts, and the rain fall in torrents, and to be sensible that Miss Miller had taken her place by my side. When I again unclosed my eyes, a loud bell was ringing; the girls were up and dressing; day had not yet begun to dawn, and a rushlight or two burned in the room. I too rose reluctantly; it was bitter cold, and I dressed as well as I could for shivering, and washed when there was a basin at liberty, which did not occur soon, as there was but one basin to six girls, on the stands down the middle of the room. Again the bell rang: all formed in file, two and two, and in that order descended the stairs and entered the cold and dimly lit schoolroom: here prayers were read by Miss Miller; afterwards she called out—

"Form classes!'"

Chapter V:

"The bread and cheese was presently brought in and distributed, to the high delight and refreshment of the whole school. The order was now given 'To the garden!' Each put on a coarse straw bonnet, with strings of coloured calico, and a cloak of grey frieze. I was similarly equipped, and, following the stream, I made my way into the open air.

"The garden was a wide inclosure, surrounded with walls so high as to exclude every glimpse of prospect; a covered verandah ran down one side, and broad walks bordered a middle space divided into scores of little beds: these beds were assigned as gardens for the pupils to cultivate, and each bed had an owner. When full of flowers they would doubtless look pretty; but now, at the latter end of January, all was wintry blight and brown decay. I shuddered as I stood and looked round me: it was an inclement day for outdoor exercise; not positively rainy, but darkened by a drizzling yellow fog; all under foot was still soaking wet with the floods of yesterday. The stronger among the girls ran about and engaged in active games, but sundry pale and thin ones herded together for shelter and warmth in the verandah; and amongst these, as the dense mist penetrated to their shivering frames, I heard frequently the sound of a hollow cough.

"As yet I had spoken to no one, nor did anybody seem to take notice of me; I stood lonely enough: but to that feeling of isolation I was accustomed; it did not oppress me much. I leant against a pillar of the verandah, drew my grey mantle close about me, and, trying to forget the cold which nipped me without, and the unsatisfied hunger which gnawed me within, delivered myself up to the employment of watching and thinking. My reflections were too undefined and fragmentary to merit record: I hardly yet knew where I was; Gateshead and my past life seemed floated away to an immeasurable distance; the present was vague and strange, and of the future I could form no conjecture. I looked round the convent-like garden, and then up at the house—a large building, half of which seemed grey and old, the other half quite new. The new part, containing the schoolroom and dormitory, was lit by mullioned and latticed windows, which gave it a church-like aspect; a stone tablet over the door bore this inscription:—

"'Lowood Institution.—This portion was rebuilt A.D. ---, by Naomi Brocklehurst, of Brocklehurst Hall, in this county.' 'Let your light so shine before men, that they may see your good works, and glorify your Father which is in heaven.'—St. Matt. v. 16."

Chapter VI:

"...the water in the pitchers was frozen. A change had taken place in the weather the preceding evening, and a keen north-east wind, whistling through the crevices of our bedroom windows all night long, had made us shiver in our beds, and turned the contents of the ewers to ice."

Chapter VI:

"...when I passed the windows, I now and then lifted a blind, and looked out; it snowed fast, a drift was already forming against the lower panes; putting my ear close to the window, I could distinguish from the gleeful tumult within, the disconsolate moan of the wind outside.

"Probably, if I had lately left a good home and kind parents, this would have been the hour when I should most keenly have regretted the separation; that wind would then have saddened my heart; this obscure chaos would have disturbed my peace! as it was, I derived from both a strange excitement, and reckless and feverish, I wished the wind to howl more wildly, the gloom to deepen to darkness, and the confusion to rise to clamour."

Chapter VII:

"During January, February, and part of March, the deep snows, and, after their melting, the almost impassable roads, prevented our stirring beyond the garden walls, except to go to church; but within these limits we had to pass an hour every day in the open air. Our clothing was insufficient to protect us from the severe cold: we had no boots, the snow got into our shoes and melted there: our ungloved hands became numbed and covered with chilblains, as were our feet: I remember well the distracting irritation I endured from this cause every evening, when my feet inflamed; and the torture of thrusting the swelled, raw, and stiff toes into my shoes in the morning. Then the scanty supply of food was distressing: with the keen appetites of growing children, we had scarcely sufficient to keep alive a delicate invalid. From this deficiency of nourishment resulted an abuse, which pressed hardly on the younger pupils: whenever the famished great girls had an opportunity, they would coax or menace the little ones out of their portion. Many a time I have shared between two claimants the precious morsel of brown bread distributed at tea-time; and after relinquishing to a third half the contents of my mug of coffee, I have swallowed the remainder with an accompaniment of secret tears, forced from me by the exigency of hunger.

"Sundays were dreary days in that wintry season. We had to walk two miles to Brocklebridge Church, where our patron officiated. We set out cold, we arrived at church colder: during the morning service we became almost paralysed. It was too far to return to dinner, and an allowance of cold meat and bread, in the same penurious proportion observed in our ordinary meals, was served round between the services.

"At the close of the afternoon service we returned by an exposed and hilly road, where the bitter winter wind, blowing over a range of snowy summits to the north, almost flayed the skin from our faces."

Chapter IX:

"But the privations, or rather the hardships, of Lowood lessened. Spring drew on: she was indeed already come; the frosts of winter had ceased; its snows were melted, its cutting winds ameliorated. My wretched feet, flayed and swollen to lameness by the sharp air of January, began to heal and subside under the gentler breathings of April; the nights and mornings no longer by their Canadian temperature froze the very blood in our veins; we could now endure the play-hour passed in the garden: sometimes on a sunny day it began even to be pleasant and genial, and a greenness grew over those brown beds, which, freshening daily, suggested the thought that Hope traversed them at night, and left each morning brighter traces of her steps. Flowers peeped out amongst the leaves; snow-drops, crocuses, purple auriculas, and golden-eyed pansies. On Thursday afternoons (half-holidays) we now took walks, and found still sweeter flowers opening by the wayside, under the hedges.

"I discovered, too, that a great pleasure, an enjoyment which the horizon only bounded, lay all outside the high and spike-guarded walls of our garden: this pleasure consisted in prospect of noble summits girdling a great hill-hollow, rich in verdure and shadow; in a bright beck, full of dark stones and sparkling eddies. How different had this scene looked when I viewed it laid out beneath the iron sky of winter, stiffened in frost, shrouded with snow!—when mists as chill as death wandered to the impulse of east winds along those purple peaks, and rolled down "ing" and holm till they blended with the frozen fog of the beck! That beck itself was then a torrent, turbid and curbless: it tore asunder the wood, and sent a raving sound through the air, often thickened with wild rain or whirling sleet; and for the forest on its banks, *that* showed only ranks of skeletons.

"April advanced to May: a bright serene May it was; days of blue sky, placid sunshine, and soft western or southern gales filled up its duration. And now vegetation matured with vigour; Lowood shook loose its tresses; it became all green, all flowery; its great elm, ash, and oak skeletons were restored to majestic life; woodland plants sprang up profusely in its recesses; unnumbered varieties of moss filled its hollows, and it made a strange ground-sunshine out of the wealth of its wild primrose plants: I have seen their pale gold gleam in overshadowed spots like scatterings of the sweetest lustre. All this I enjoyed often and fully, free, unwatched, and almost alone: for this unwonted liberty and pleasure there was a cause, to which it now becomes my task to advert.

"Have I not described a pleasant site for a dwelling, when I speak of it as bosomed in hill and wood, and rising from the verge of a stream? Assuredly, pleasant enough: but whether healthy or not is another question.

"That forest-dell, where Lowood lay, was the cradle of fog and fog-bred pestilence; which, quickening with the quickening spring, crept into the Orphan Asylum, breathed typhus through its crowded schoolroom and dormitory, and, ere May arrived, transformed the seminary into an hospital.

"Semi-starvation and neglected colds had predisposed most of the pupils to receive infection: forty-five out of the eighty girls lay ill at one time. Classes were broken up, rules relaxed. The few who continued well were allowed almost unlimited license; because the medical attendant insisted on the necessity of frequent exercise to keep them in health: and had it been otherwise, no one had leisure to watch or restrain them. Miss Temple's whole attention was absorbed by the patients: she lived in the sick-room, never quitting it except to snatch a few hours' rest at night. The teachers were fully occupied with packing up and making other necessary preparations for the departure of those girls who were fortunate enough to have friends and relations able and willing to remove them from the seat of contagion. Many, already smitten, went home only to die: some died at the school, and were buried quietly and quickly, the nature of the malady forbidding delay.

"While disease had thus become an inhabitant of Lowood, and death its frequent visitor; while there was gloom and fear within its walls; while its rooms and passages steamed with hospital smells, the drug and the pastille striving vainly to overcome the effluvia of mortality, that bright May shone unclouded over the bold hills and beautiful woodland out of doors. Its garden, too, glowed with flowers: hollyhocks had sprung up tall as trees, lilies had opened, tulips and roses were in bloom; the borders of the little beds were gay with pink thrift and crimson double daisies; the sweetbriars gave out, morning and evening, their scent of spice and apples; and these fragrant treasures were all useless for most of the inmates of Lowood, except to furnish now and then a handful of herbs and blossoms to put in a coffin."

Chapter XI:

"A new chapter in a novel is something like a new scene in a play; and when I draw up the curtain this time, reader, you must fancy you see a room in the George Inn at Millcote, with such large figured papering on the walls as inn rooms have; such a carpet, such furniture, such ornaments on the mantelpiece, such prints, including a portrait of George the Third, and another of the Prince of Wales, and a representation of the death of Wolfe. All this is visible to you by the light of an oil lamp hanging from the ceiling, and by that of an excellent fire, near which I sit in my cloak and bonnet; my muff and umbrella lie on the table, and I am warming away the numbness and chill contracted by sixteen hours' exposure to the rawness of an October day: I left Lowton at four o'clock a.m., and the Millcote town clock is now just striking eight."

Chapter XI:

"The hall-door, which was half of glass, stood open; I stepped over the threshold. It was a fine autumn morning; the early sun shone serenely on embrowned groves and still green fields; advancing on to the lawn, I looked up and surveyed the front of the mansion. It was three storeys high, of proportions not vast, though considerable: a gentleman's manor-house, not a nobleman's seat: battlements round the top gave it a picturesque look. Its grey front stood out well from the background of a rookery, whose cawing tenants were now on the wing: they flew over the lawn and grounds to alight in a great meadow, from which these were separated by a sunk fence, and where an array of mighty old thorn trees, strong, knotty, and broad as oaks, at once explained the etymology of the mansion's designation. Farther off were hills: not so lofty as those round Lowood, nor so craggy, nor so like barriers of separation from the living world; but yet quiet and lonely hills enough, and seeming to embrace Thornfield with a seclusion I had not expected to find existent so near the stirring locality of Millcote. A little hamlet, whose roofs were blent with trees, straggled up the side of one of these hills; the church of the district stood nearer Thornfield: its old tower-top looked over a knoll between the house and gates."

Chapter XII:

"October, November, December passed away. One afternoon in January, Mrs. Fairfax had begged a holiday for Adèle, because she had a cold; and, as Adèle seconded the request with an ardour that reminded me how precious occasional holidays had been to me in my own childhood, I accorded it, deeming that I did well in showing pliability on the point. It was a fine, calm day, though very cold; I was tired of sitting still in the library through a whole long morning: Mrs. Fairfax had just written a letter which was waiting to be posted, so I put on my bonnet and cloak and volunteered to carry it to Hay; the distance, two miles, would be a pleasant winter afternoon walk. Having seen Adèle comfortably seated in her little chair by Mrs. Fairfax's parlour fireside, and given her her best wax doll (which I usually kept enveloped in silver paper in a drawer) to play with, and a story-book for change of amusement; and having replied to her 'Revenez bientôt, ma bonne amie, ma chère Mdlle. Jeannette,' with a kiss I set out.

"The ground was hard, the air was still, my road was lonely; I walked fast till I got warm, and then I walked slowly to enjoy and analyse the species of pleasure brooding for me in the hour and situation. It was three o'clock; the church bell tolled as I passed under the belfry: the charm of the hour lay in its approaching dimness, in the low-gliding and pale-beaming sun. I was a mile from Thornfield, in a lane noted for wild roses in summer, for nuts and blackberries in autumn, and even now possessing a few coral treasures in hips and haws, but whose best winter delight lay in its utter solitude and leafless repose. If a breath of air stirred, it made no sound here; for there was not a holly, not an evergreen to rustle, and the stripped hawthorn and hazel bushes were as still as the white, worn stones which causewayed the middle of the path. Far and wide, on each side, there were only fields, where no cattle now browsed; and the little brown birds, which stirred occasionally in the hedge, looked like single russet leaves that had forgotten to drop.

"This lane inclined up-hill all the way to Hay; having reached the middle, I sat down on a stile which led thence into a field. Gathering my mantle about me, and sheltering my hands in my muff, I did not feel the cold, though it froze keenly; as was attested by a sheet of ice covering the causeway, where a little brooklet, now congealed, had overflowed after a rapid thaw some days since. From my seat I could look down on Thornfield: the grey and battlemented hall was the principal object in the vale below me; its woods and dark rookery rose against the west. I lingered till the sun went down amongst the trees, and sank crimson and clear behind them. I then turned eastward.

"On the hill-top above me sat the rising moon; pale yet as a cloud, but brightening momentarily, she looked over Hay, which, half lost in trees, sent up a blue smoke from its few chimneys: it was yet a mile distant, but in the absolute hush I could hear plainly its thin murmurs of life. My ear, too, felt the flow of currents; in what dales and depths I could not tell: but there were many hills beyond Hay, and doubtless many becks threading their passes. That evening calm betrayed alike the tinkle of the nearest streams, the sough of the most remote.

"A rude noise broke on these fine ripplings and whisperings, at once so far away and so clear: a positive tramp, tramp, a metallic clatter, which effaced the soft wave-wanderings; as, in a picture, the solid mass of a crag, or the rough boles of a great oak, drawn in dark and strong on the foreground, efface the aërial distance of azure hill, sunny horizon, and blended clouds where tint melts into tint."

Chapter XII:

"I had it still before me when I entered Hay, and slipped the letter into the post-office; I saw it as I walked fast down-hill all the way home. When I came to the stile, I stopped a minute, looked round and listened, with an idea that a horse's hoofs might ring on the causeway again, and that a rider in a cloak, and a Gytrash-like Newfoundland dog, might be again apparent: I saw only the hedge and a pollard willow before me, rising up still and straight to meet the moonbeams; I heard only the faintest waft of wind roaming fitful among the trees round Thornfield, a mile distant; and when I glanced down in the direction of the murmur, my eye, traversing the hall-front, caught a light kindling in a window: it reminded me that I was late, and I hurried on."

Chapter XVIII:

"The kitchen, the butler's pantry, the servants' hall, the entrance hall, were equally alive; and the saloons were only left void and still when the blue sky and halcyon sunshine of the genial spring weather called their occupants out into the grounds. Even when that weather was broken, and continuous rain set in for some days, no damp seemed cast over enjoyment: indoor amusements only became more lively and varied, in consequence of the stop put to outdoor gaiety."

Chapter XX:

"He strayed down a walk edged with box, with apple trees, pear trees, and cherry trees on one side, and a border on the other full of all sorts of old-fashioned flowers, stocks, sweet-williams, primroses, pansies, mingled with southernwood, sweet-briar, and various fragrant herbs. They were fresh now as a succession of April showers and gleams, followed by a lovely spring morning, could make them: the sun was just entering the dappled east, and his light illumined the wreathed and dewy orchard trees and shone down the quiet walks under them."

Chapter XXIII:

"A splendid Midsummer shone over England: skies so pure, suns so radiant as were then seen in long succession, seldom favour even singly, our wave-girt land. It was as if a band of Italian days had come from the South, like a flock of glorious passenger birds, and lighted to rest them on the cliffs of Albion. The hay was all got in; the fields round Thornfield were green and shorn; the roads white and baked; the trees were in their dark prime; hedge and wood, full-leaved and deeply tinted, contrasted well with the sunny hue of the cleared meadows between.

"On Midsummer-eve, Adèle, weary with gathering wild strawberries in Hay Lane half the day, had gone to bed with the sun. I watched her drop asleep, and when I left her, I sought the garden.

"It was now the sweetest hour of the twenty-four:—'Day its fervid fires had wasted,'"and dew fell cool on panting plain and scorched summit. Where the sun had gone down in simple state—pure of the pomp of clouds—spread a solemn purple, burning with the light of red jewel and furnace flame at one point, on one hill-peak, and extending high and wide, soft and still softer, over half heaven. The east had its own charm or fine deep blue, and its own modest gem, a casino and solitary star: soon it would boast the moon; but she was yet beneath the horizon."

Chapter XXVI:

"Jane Eyre, who had been an ardent, expectant woman—almost a bride, was a cold, solitary girl again: her life was pale; her prospects were desolate. A Christmas frost had come at midsummer; a white December storm had whirled over June; ice glazed the ripe apples, drifts crushed the blowing roses; on hayfield and cornfield lay a frozen shroud: lanes which last night blushed full of flowers, to-day were pathless with untrodden snow; and the woods, which twelve hours since waved leafy and flagrant as groves between the tropics, now spread, waste, wild, and white as pine-forests in wintry Norway."

Chapter XXVIII:

"I touched the heath: it was dry, and yet warm with the heat of the summer day. I looked at the sky; it was pure: a kindly star twinkled just above the chasm ridge. The dew fell, but with propitious softness; no breeze whispered. Nature seemed to me benign and good; I thought she loved me, outcast as I was; and I, who from man could anticipate only mistrust, rejection, insult, clung to her with filial fondness. To-night, at least, I would be her guest, as I was her child: my mother would lodge me without money and without price. I had one morsel of bread yet: the remnant of a roll I had bought in a town we passed through at noon with a stray penny—my last coin. I saw ripe bilberries gleaming here and there, like jet beads in the heath: I gathered a handful and ate them with the bread. My hunger, sharp before, was, if not satisfied, appeased by this hermit's meal. I said my evening prayers at its conclusion, and then chose my couch."

Assessment Ideas:

This activity can be collected and graded for completion, and can be used to gauge students' understanding of weather's function in the novel.

Day 5 - Reading Assignment, Questions, Vocabulary

Read *Jane Eyre,* Chapters XXXIII-XXXVIII. (These chapters can be split up as needed between reading in class and reading at home.)

Common Core Objectives

- CCSS.ELA-LITERACY.RL.11-12.1
  Cite strong and thorough textual evidence to support analysis of what the text says explicitly as well as inferences drawn from the text, including determining where the text leaves matters uncertain.

- CCSS.ELA-LITERACY.RL.11-12.2
  Determine two or more themes or central ideas of a text and analyze their development over the course of the text, including how they interact and build on one another to produce a complex account; provide an objective summary of the text.

- CCSS.ELA-Literacy.RL.11-12.7
  Analyze multiple interpretations of a story, drama, or poem (e.g., recorded or live production of a play or recorded novel or poetry), evaluating how each version interprets the source text. (Include at least one play by Shakespeare and one play by an American dramatist.)

- CCSS.ELA-Literacy.SL.11-12.3
  Evaluate a speaker's point of view, reasoning, and use of evidence and rhetoric, assessing the stance, premises, links among ideas, word choice, points of emphasis, and tone used.

Note that it is perfectly fine to expand any day's work into two days depending on the characteristics of the class, particularly if the class will engage in all of the suggested classroom exercises and activities and discuss all of the thought questions.

Content Summary for Teachers

Chapter XXXIII

St. John informs Jane that he has figured out her identity—that she is not Jane Elliott, but rather Jane Eyre. Jane Eyre, he says, has inherited twenty thousand pounds from her uncle John Eyre, who has died—and Jane's uncle is also his uncle, the same uncle who left the Rivers siblings thirty guineas and the rest to "another relative." Jane is thrilled to know that St. John, Diana, and Mary are her cousins, and because she is so delighted to have family, she decides to split her twenty thousand pounds with them equally four ways.

Chapter XXXIV

Jane closes up the school for Christmas, and at Moor House, she and Hannah prepare for the arrival of Diana and Mary. Talking to St. John, Jane realizes he is right about his own character—that he is aspirational and restless. There is a coldness in him that Jane thinks might make him a difficult husband, even for Rosamond Oliver, but she thinks that he will thrive on challenges in the future. Diana and Mary arrive, and St. John leaves to tend to a parishoner, not returning until midnight. Over the next week, St. John often spends time away visiting the people in his parish. He tells his sisters that his plans to be a missionary are unchanged, and that Rosamond Oliver is going to be married to Mr. Granby, the grandson and heir of Sir Frederic Granby. Over the next few weeks, the Rivers siblings and Jane spend time around the house, Diana reading and Jane learning German; however, St. John often encourages Jane to come on walks with him, and praises her boldness and robustness. Soon, St. John asks Jane to help him with his "Hindostanee" language studies.

Jane writes to Mr. Briggs asking for news of Mr. Rochester, but Mr. Briggs respons that he has none. She then writes to Mrs. Fairfax about Mr. Rochester and waits for a response. In the meantime, St. John plans for his missonary journey to India. Then, to Jane's surprise, St. John proposes marriage to Jane—he wants her to come with him and support his missionary work. She tells him that she would go with him, but in a sisterly capacity or as a colleague rather than as a wife. St. John is hurt, and treats Jane coldly.

Chapter XXXV

St. John defers his departure; he continues to be cold to Jane, upset at her steadfast refusal to marry him. The coldness between them is noticeable to Diana, who discusses it with Jane. After a week goes by, St. John tells Jane that he wants to do God's duty, that he will travel to Cambridge and be back in two weeks, and that he will then ask her again for her answer to his proposal. She tells him that, if she really senses that it is God's will, she will marry him, but when she prays, she believes that she hears Mr. Rochester calling her name.

Chapter XXXVI

St. John leaves for Cambridge. Jane, still shaken by Rochester's voice, leaves Diana and Mary behind and departs for Thornfield Hall. She finds Thornfield in ruins, seemingly as a result of a fire. At a nearby inn, Jane learns that nobody has lived at Thornfield since it burned down, and that Mr. Rochester's wife set the fire. From the other guest at the inn, a former butler to the Rochester family, Jane hears her own story, of Mr. Rochester's love for her and desire to marry her. Jane learns that, after a futile search for her, Mr. Rochester had become hermit-like, sending Mrs. Fairfax away with an annuity and sending Adèle to school. The night Mr. Rochester's wife set the fire, he made sure the servants were safe, and then went back for his wife, who was on the roof. He called out to her, and she jumped off the roof to her death. Mr. Rochester was badly injured in the fire, losing both his hand and his eyesight. He now lives at Ferndean, "a manor-house on a farm he has."

Chapter XXXVII

Jane goes to Ferndean. When she sees Mr. Rochester, she is taken once again with love; she tells him that she will not leave him. Mr. Rochester is worried that she is revolted by him, but she says that she is not. At his request, she relates the story of the past year of her life, including her inheritance and her relationship with St. John. When Mr. Rochester finally understands that Jane still loves him, he asks Jane to marry him, and she accepts. He tells her that he called out, "Jane! Jane! Jane!" just as Jane thought she heard when she prayed with St. John, and that he heard her response.

Chapter XXXVIII

Jane marries Mr. Rochester in a quiet ceremony. St. John never writes a response to Jane's letter telling news of her marriage, but he does occasionally write to her. Jane takes Adèle out of a school that is overly severe, wanting at first to teach her at home again, and then finds another, more suitable school for Adèle where Jane can visit her often.

At the end of the novel, Jane and Mr. Rochester have been married for ten years. Diana and Mary are both happily married. St. John is unmarried and has devoted himself to his missionary work. Mr. Rochester regains his sight in one eye and is happy to be able to see his first-born child.

Thought Questions (students consider while they read)

1. Should St. John have married Rosamond Oliver?

2. How does Jane feel about marriage without love?

3. Why does Jane opt to share the money she inherits?

4. How does Jane feel about her students at the school in Morton?

5. Are you satisfied with the ending of *Jane Eyre*?

Vocabulary (in order of appearance)

Chapter XXXIII: ...no vestige of information could be gathered respecting her.

vestige:

a trace left by something that has disappeared, is disappearing, or is lost

Chapter XXXIII: This was a blessing, bright, vivid, and exhilarating;—not like the ponderous gift of gold: rich and welcome enough in its way, but sobering from its weight.

ponderous:

heavy, cumbersome

Chapter XXXIII: ...in your conversation I have already for some time found a salutary solace.

salutary:

good for health, having a beneficial effect

Chapter XXXIV: ...she was charmed to see how jovial I could be amidst the bustle of a house turned topsy-turvy—how I could brush, and dust, and clean, and cook.

jovial:

friendly and cheerful, jolly

Chapter XXXIV: I inquired whether this was the case: no doubt in a somewhat crestfallen tone.

crestfallen:

disappointed, dejected, discouraged

Chapter XXXIV: They could always talk; and their discourse, witty, pithy, original, had such charms for me, that I preferred listening to, and sharing in it, to doing anything else.

pithy:

effective in expression with few words, concise, cogent

Chapter XXXIV: Diana, who chanced to be in a frolicsome humour (she was not painfully controlled by his will; for hers, in another way, was as strong), exclaimed—

frolicsome:

playful and lively

Chapter XXXIV: Not his ascendancy alone, however, held me in thrall at present.

ascendancy:

a position of power and influence

thrall:

a state of captivity

Chapter XXXIV: ...stringent are they...

stringent:

exacting, strict, precise, rigorous

Chapter XXXIV: for you I have only a comrade's constancy; a fellow-soldier's frankness, fidelity, fraternity, if you like; a neophyte's respect and submission to his hierophant: nothing more—don't fear."

hierophant:

a person who explains sacred mysteries

Chapter XXXIV: "I scorn the counterfeit sentiment you offer: yes, St. John, and I scorn you when you offer it."

counterfeit:

in fraudulent imitation

Chapter XXXIV: Whether he was incensed or surprised, or what, it was not easy to tell: he could command his countenance thoroughly.

incensed:

very angry

Chapter XXXIV: I was touched by his gentle tone, and overawed by his high, calm mien.

overawed:

rendered speechless from being awed, respectful, or fearful

Chapter XXXV: He deferred his departure a whole week, and during that time he made me feel what severe punishment a good yet stern, a conscientious yet implacable man can inflict on one who has offended him.

implacable:

unable to be pacified or appeased

Chapter XXXV: What struggle there was in him between Nature and Grace in this interval, I cannot tell: only singular gleams scintillated in his eyes, and strange shadows passed over his face.

scintillated:

sparkled, emitted sparks or flashes of light

Chapter XXXV: Anything like a tangible reproach gave me courage at once.

tangible:

able to be sensed by touch, definite, real or actual

Chapter XXXV: It was at all times pleasant to listen while from his lips fell the words of the Bible: never did his fine voice sound at once so sweet and full—never did his manner become so impressive in its noble simplicity, as when he delivered the oracles of God...

oracles:

divine communications or prophecies, people through whom a deity speaks, shrines for a deity to reveal knowledge

Chapter XXXV: I cannot give you up to perdition as a vessel of wrath: repent—resolve, while there is yet time.

perdition:

eternal punishment after death

Chapter XXXVI: No wonder that letters addressed to people here had never received an answer: as well despatch epistles to a vault in a church aisle.

epistles:

compositions written in letter format

Chapter XXXVI: In wandering round the shattered walls and through the devastated interior, I gathered evidence that the calamity was not of late occurrence.

calamity:

a disaster, an event causing great damage

Chapter XXXVI: He sent Mrs. Fairfax, the housekeeper, away to her friends at a distance; but he did it handsomely, for he settled an annuity on her for life: and she deserved it—she was a very good woman.

annuity:

a set sum of money provided for someone each year

Chapter XXXVII: The darkness of natural as well as of sylvan dusk gathered over me.

sylvan:

having to do with the woods or the forest

Chapter XXXVII: "I thought you would be revolted, Jane, when you saw my arm, and my cicatrised visage."

cicatrised:

scarred, healed by scar tissue

Chapter XXXVII: "Very dimly—each is a luminous cloud."

luminous:

shining, bright, full of light

Chapter XXXVII: If Saul could have had you for his David, the evil spirit would have been exorcised without the aid of the harp.

exorcised:

driven out, gotten rid of

Chapter XXXVII: It was mournful, indeed, to witness the subjugation of that vigorous spirit to a corporeal infirmity.

subjugation:

defeating and gaining control of something or someone

corporeal:

having to do with the body

Chapter XXXVII: A person whose goodness consists rather in his guiltlessness of vice, than in his prowess in virtue.

prowess:

skill, bravery, expertise

Chapter XXXVII: "That is a fiction—an impudent invention to vex me."

impudent:

not showing respect, brazen

Additional Homework

1. Students should find two reviews of the 2011 film adaptation of *Jane Eyre*. For each review, the students should write down answers to the following questions:

1. What points does the reviewer make that you agree with? Why do you agree?

2. What points does the reviewer make that you disagree with? Why do you disagree?

3. What new realizations did you have about the film and/or the novel as a result of reading this review?

Day 5 - Discussion of Thought Questions

1. Should St. John have married Rosamond Oliver?

Time:

5 minutes

Discussion:

Some students may think that he might have found married happiness with someone he loved, but others may believe that marrying her could have ruined both of their lives because, despite loving her, he might have always longed for missionary work somewhere far away. There may be still other students who believe that Rosamond Oliver could have adjusted to the life of a missionary, although she was accustomed to wealth and missionary work would be a life of deprivation.

2. How does Jane feel about marriage without love?

Time:

5 minutes

Discussion:

For Jane, love is essential to a marriage. She would rather be unmarried than marry for any other reason. For instance, Jane does not want to marry St. John because she does not love him and knows that he does not love her, either, but, rather, recognizes qualities in her that will be helpful to him in his missionary work. She sees friendship as a viable alternative, but St. John does not.

3. Why does Jane opt to share the money she inherits?

Time:

5 minutes

Discussion:

Jane is grateful to have cousins, after a lifetime feeling lonely and isolated without family, and she wants to keep her cousins close by sharing her money with them. Also, this is a way in which she can help her cousins, who have shown her a great deal of kindness. They also were set to inherit money from the same uncle, but only inherit thirty guineas between them, and could use the money.

4. How does Jane feel about her students at the school in Morton?

Time:

5 minutes

Discussion:

At first, Jane does not have high expectations for her students, and expects to tolerate but not love her job teaching them. Students should tease out the meaning of these expectations—Jane does not expect that village or peasant children would have the same capacity to learn as other girls she has known. However, gradually, she grows to understand her students and to appreciate and like them.

5. Are you satisfied with the ending of *Jane Eyre*?

Time:

5 minutes

Discussion:

Students may have felt invested in the romance between Jane Eyre and Mr. Rochester, and thus will be delighted that the two find their way back to each other, even though they may feel bad about Mr. Rochester's condition. They may be happy for Diana and Mary, and some may be glad that St. John got what he wanted, though others may wonder about his choice not to marry. Other students may feel that the story ends a little too "perfectly," with love ultimately conquering all.

Day 5 - Short Answer Evaluation

1. What does Jane do with the money she inherits?

   _____

2. What job do Diana and Mary Rivers have?

   _____

3. How are Diana, Mary, and St. John Rivers related to Jane?

   _____

4. What job does Jane have in Morton?

   _____

5. What does St. John yearn to do for work, and does he ever do it?

   _____

6. What does Jane think she hears the night before St. John leaves for Cambridge?

   _____

7. What happens to Adèle?

   _____

8. Whom does St. John want to marry and bring to India?

   _____

9. To whom is Jane married at the end of the novel?

10. What happens to Mrs. Fairfax?

Answer Key

1. She shares it equally with St. John, Mary, and Diana Rivers.
2. They both work as governesses.
3. They are Jane's cousins. Jane's uncle John Eyre is also their uncle.
4. She is the schoolmistress at the school for girls that St. John opens.
5. He wants to become a missionary and eventually goes to India to do missionary work.
6. She thinks she hears Mr. Rochester calling her name.
7. She is sent to a school which Jane deems too severe, then sent to another, more suitable school where Jane can visit her often.
8. St. John wants to bring Jane to India with him as his wife.
9. Jane is married to Mr. Rochester at the end of the novel.
10. Mr. Rochester sends her away to her friends and provides her with an annuity.

Day 5 - Crossword Puzzle

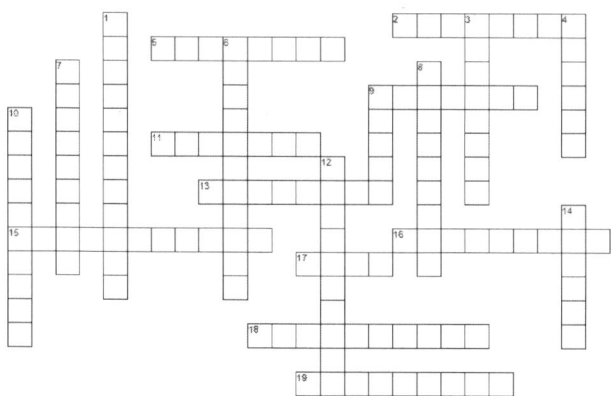

ACROSS

2. Shining, bright, full of light
5. Compositions written in letter format
9. Skill, bravery, expertise
11. Mrs. Fairfax receives an _____.
13. A disaster, an event causing great damage
15. In fraudulent imitation
16. Eternal punishment after death
17. St. _____ proposes to Jane.
18. Scarred, healed by scar tissue
19. Exacting, strict, precise, rigorous

DOWN

1. Sparkled, emitted sparks or flashes of light
3. Very angry
4. Having to do with the woods or the forest
6. Defeating and gaining control of something or someone

7. Heavy, cumbersome
8. Jane marries Mr. _____.
9. Effective in expression with few words, concise, cogent

10. Unable to be pacified or appeased
12. A person who explains sacred mysteries
14. Friendly and cheerful, jolly

Crossword Puzzle Answer Key

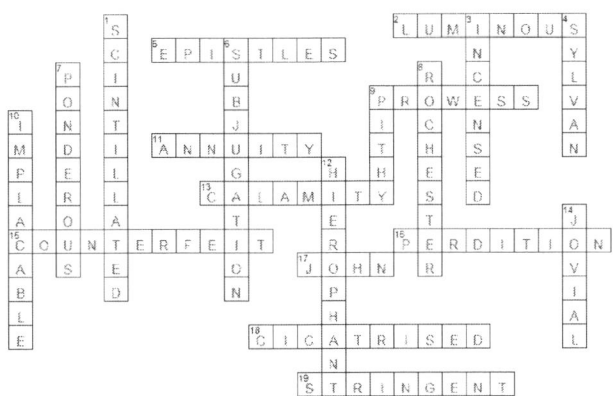

ACROSS

2. Shining, bright, full of light
5. Compositions written in letter format
9. Skill, bravery, expertise
11. Mrs. Fairfax receives an _____
13. A disaster, an event causing great damage
15. In fraudulent imitation
16. Eternal punishment after death
17. St. _____ proposes to Jane
18. Scarred, healed by scar tissue
19. Exacting, strict, precise, rigorous

DOWN

1. Sparkled, emitted sparks or flashes of light
3. Very angry
4. Having to do with the woods or the forest
6. Defeating and gaining control of something or someone
7. Heavy, cumbersome
8. Jane marries Mr. _____
9. Effective in expression with few words, concise, cogent
10. Unable to be pacified or appeased
12. A person who explains sacred mysteries
14. Friendly and cheerful, jolly

Day 5 - Vocabulary Quiz

Terms

1. _____ ponderous
2. _____ salutary
3. _____ prowess
4. _____ calamity
5. _____ incensed
6. _____ vestige
7. _____ stringent
8. _____ annuity
9. _____ sylvan
10. _____ impudent
11. _____ jovial
12. _____ counterfeit
13. _____ overawed
14. _____ implacable
15. _____ perdition
16. _____ scintillated
17. _____ exorcised
18. _____ tangible
19. _____ frolicsome
20. _____ oracles

Answers

A. sparkled, emitted sparks or flashes of light
B. eternal punishment after death
C. able to be sensed by touch, definite, real or actual
D. rendered speechless from being awed, respectful, or fearful
E. good for health, having a beneficial effect
F. in fraudulent imitation
G. driven out, gotten rid of
H. skill, bravery, expertise
I. exacting, strict, precise, rigorous
J. heavy, cumbersome
K. a set sum of money provided for someone each year
L. a trace left by something that has disappeared, is disappearing, or is lost
M. divine communications or prophecies, people through whom a deity speaks, shrines for a deity to reveal knowledge
N. having to do with the woods or the forest
O. friendly and cheerful, jolly
P. unable to be pacified or appeased
Q. a disaster, an event causing great damage
R. playful and lively
S. not showing respect, brazen
T. very angry

Answer Key

1. J ponderous: heavy, cumbersome
2. E salutary: good for health, having a beneficial effect
3. H prowess: skill, bravery, expertise
4. Q calamity: a disaster, an event causing great damage
5. T incensed: very angry
6. L vestige: a trace left by something that has disappeared, is disappearing, or is lost
7. I stringent: exacting, strict, precise, rigorous
8. K annuity: a set sum of money provided for someone each year
9. N sylvan: having to do with the woods or the forest
10. S impudent: not showing respect, brazen
11. O jovial: friendly and cheerful, jolly
12. F counterfeit: in fraudulent imitation
13. D overawed: rendered speechless from being awed, respectful, or fearful
14. P implacable: unable to be pacified or appeased
15. B perdition: eternal punishment after death
16. A scintillated: sparkled, emitted sparks or flashes of light
17. G exorcised: driven out, gotten rid of
18. C tangible: able to be sensed by touch, definite, real or actual
19. R frolicsome: playful and lively
20. M oracles: divine communications or prophecies, people through whom a deity speaks, shrines for a deity to reveal knowledge

Day 5 - Classroom Activities

1. Jane Eyre Illustration Design

Kind of Activity:

Artistic Response

Objective:

Students will create illustrations for Jane Eyre.

Common Core Standards:

CCSS.ELA-LITERACY.RL.11-12.2

Time:

45 minutes

Structure:

1. As a class, students should brainstorm what important elements from the novel could be brought out with illustrations. Refer to Brontë's complex, often lush visual descriptions.

2. Project Gutenberg contains a copy of *Jane Eyre* transcribed from the 1897 Service & Paton edition by David Price. It contains illustrations by F.H. Townsend. In pairs, students should look at and discuss some of these illustrations. Do they feel that the illustrations capture the characters and events well? If so, what elements of the art make it successful? If not, what do the students feel is missing, or could be changed?

3. Students should create their own illustrations for excerpts from the novel. Students should include with their illustrations 1-2 paragraph descriptions explaining the choices they made and what about the book they wanted to represent.

Ideas for Differentiated Instruction:

can give students a choice of specific passages to illustrate. Some sages are:

Chapter I:

"Folds of scarlet drapery shut in my view to the right hand; to the left were the clear panes of glass, protecting, but not separating me from the drear November day. At intervals, while turning over the leaves of my book, I studied the aspect of that winter afternoon. Afar, it offered a pale blank of mist and cloud; near a scene of wet lawn and storm-beat shrub, with ceaseless rain sweeping away wildly before a long and lamentable blast."

Chapter IX:

"April advanced to May: a bright serene May it was; days of blue sky, placid sunshine, and soft western or southern gales filled up its duration. And now vegetation matured with vigour; Lowood shook loose its tresses; it became all green, all flowery; its great elm, ash, and oak skeletons were restored to majestic life; woodland plants sprang up profusely in its recesses; unnumbered varieties of moss filled its hollows, and it made a strange ground-sunshine out of the wealth of its wild primrose plants: I have seen their pale gold gleam in overshadowed spots like scatterings of the sweetest lustre. All this I enjoyed often and fully, free, unwatched, and almost alone: for this unwonted liberty and pleasure there was a cause, to which it now becomes my task to advert."

Chapter X:

"With earliest day, I was up: I had my advertisement written, enclosed, and directed before the bell rang to rouse the school; it ran thus:—

"'A young lady accustomed to tuition' (had I not been a teacher two years?) 'is desirous of meeting with a situation in a private family where the children are under fourteen' (I thought that as I was barely eighteen, it would not do to undertake the guidance of pupils nearer my own age). 'She is qualified to teach the usual branches of a good English education, together with French, Drawing, and Music' (in those days, reader, this now narrow catalogue of accomplishments, would have been held tolerably comprehensive). 'Address, J.E., Post-office, Lowton, ---shire.'"

Chapter XI:

"Again I looked out: we were passing a church; I saw its low broad tower against the sky, and its bell was tolling a quarter; I saw a narrow galaxy of lights too, on a hillside, marking a village or hamlet."

Chapter XI:

"A snug small room; a round table by a cheerful fire; an arm-chair high-backed and old-fashioned, wherein sat the neatest imaginable little elderly lady, in widow's cap, black silk gown, and snowy muslin apron; exactly like what I had fancied Mrs. Fairfax, only less stately and milder looking. She was occupied in knitting; a large cat sat demurely at her feet; nothing in short was wanting to complete the beau-ideal of domestic comfort."

Chapter XI:

"Traversing the long and matted gallery, I descended the slippery steps of oak; then I gained the hall: I halted there a minute; I looked at some pictures on the walls (one, I remember, represented a grim man in a cuirass, and one a lady with powdered hair and a pearl necklace), at a bronze lamp pendent from the ceiling, at a great clock whose case was of oak curiously carved, and ebon black with time and rubbing. Everything appeared very stately and imposing to me; but then I was so little accustomed to grandeur. The hall-door, which was half of glass, stood open; I stepped over the threshold. It was a fine autumn morning; the early sun shone serenely on embrowned groves and still green fields; advancing on to the lawn, I looked up and surveyed the front of the mansion. It was three storeys high, of proportions not vast, though considerable: a gentleman's manor-house, not a nobleman's seat: battlements round the top gave it a picturesque look. Its grey front stood out well from the background of a rookery, whose cawing tenants were now on the wing: they flew over the lawn and grounds to alight in a great meadow, from which these were separated by a sunk fence, and where an array of mighty old thorn trees, strong, knotty, and broad as oaks, at once explained the etymology of the mansion's designation. Farther off were hills: not so lofty as those round Lowood, nor so craggy, nor so like barriers of separation from the living world; but yet quiet and lonely hills enough, and seeming to embrace Thornfield with a seclusion I had not expected to find existent so near the stirring locality of Millcote. A little hamlet, whose roofs were blent with trees, straggled up the side of one of these hills; the church of the district stood nearer Thornfield: its old tower-top looked over a knoll between the house and gates."

Assessment Ideas:

Teachers can use the explanations the students write to understand students' thinking process about the novel and about the illustrations that the students have made. The illustrations should also be assessed on completeness and artistic complexity.

2. Interviews with Characters from Jane Eyre about the 2011 Film Adaptation

Kind of Activity:

Individual Writing

Objective:

Students will watch and review the 2011 film adaptation of Jane Eyre from the perspectives of characters from the novel.

Common Core Standards:

CCSS.ELA-LITERACY.RL.11-12.1; CCSS.ELA-Literacy.RL.11-12.7; CCSS.ELA-Literacy.SL.11-12.3

Time:

2.5 hours

Structure:

1. When students arrive, they should begin working on the following writing assignment:

Choose a character from *Jane Eyre*. From that character's point of view, answer the following questions:

If someone were making a movie of your life, who would you want to be cast as you?

What important things about your life/events in your life should be included?

How would you want to be remembered?

2. Students should discuss their responses to the questions they wrote about in pairs, and then share out their findings with the class.

3. Students should then watch the 2011 film adaptation of *Jane Eyre*, taking notes throughout the play on aspects of the film that concern or include their chosen characters.

4. After watching the movie, students should gather or be placed in pairs or small groups. In these groups, students can practice acting out an interview with the character(s) from the novel. One person can play the interviewer and the other student(s) can be the *Jane Eyre* character(s). Attempt to group the students so that all members of the group are playing different characters.

5. Students can perform their interviews for the class.

Ideas for Differentiated Instruction:

This activity could also be done as a whole-class activity, with all of the students functioning as participants in a talk show. Roles such as host, audience members, and various *Jane Eyre* characters can be assigned in advance, and students can watch the film with these roles in mind, taking notes on the film to prepare themselves.

Students can also write reviews of the 2011 film version of *Jane Eyre* from the perspective of their chosen characters after watching the film, as a way of synthesizing their thoughts.

Assessment Ideas:

Film reviews can be graded on the following criteria:

-evidence of understanding of *Jane Eyre*

-evidence of understanding of students' chosen characters

-cogent analysis of choices made by the film's director about how to bring the novel to the screen

-grammar and mechanics

-organization

Interview presentations can be graded on the following criteria:

-understanding of the characters

-completion of task

-group cooperation

-comparison of film to text

Day 6 - Reading Assignment, Questions, Vocabulary

Read the Preface to the Second Edition and Note to the Third Edition of *Jane Eyre*. (These can be read in class or at home.)

Common Core Objectives

- CCSS.ELA-Literacy.RL.11-12.10

  By the end of grade 11, read and comprehend literature, including stories, dramas, and poems, in the grades 11-CCR text complexity band proficiently, with scaffolding as needed at the high end of the range.

  By the end of grade 12, read and comprehend literature, including stories, dramas, and poems, at the high end of the grades 11-CCR text complexity band independently and proficiently.

- CCSS.ELA-Literacy.W.11-12.3
  Write narratives to develop real or imagined experiences or events using effective technique, well-chosen details, and well-structured event sequences.

- CCSS.ELA-Literacy.W.11-12.6
  Use technology, including the Internet, to produce, publish, and update individual or shared writing products in response to ongoing feedback, including new arguments or information.

- CCSS.ELA-Literacy.SL.11-12.1
  Initiate and participate effectively in a range of collaborative discussions (one-on-one, in groups, and teacher-led) with diverse partners on grades 11-12 topics, texts, and issues, building on others' ideas and expressing their own clearly and persuasively.

Note that it is perfectly fine to expand any day's work into two days depending on the characteristics of the class, particularly if the class will engage in all of the suggested classroom exercises and activities and discuss all of the thought questions.

Content Summary for Teachers

Preface to the Second Edition

Charlotte Brontë, writing under the name of Currer Bell, thanks the Press, the Public, and the Publishers for their support. She then turns to her detractors and doubters.

She thanks her supporters for their openness and generosity. To her critics, she presents the idea that rigid adherence to conventionality, self-righteousness, or "narrow human doctrines" is not the same as morality or religion. While it is easy to complacently accept "external show" to pass for "sterling worth," ultimately, the world is grateful to those who dig beneath the surface. She claims that one such writer who digs beneath the surface is Thackeray, to whom she dedicates the second edition of *Jane Eyre*.

Note to the Third Edition

In the note to the third edition, Currer Bell explains that Bell's claim to authorship can only be valid for *Jane Eyre*. Bell states that attributions of Bell's authorship to other works of fiction denies credit to the actual authors of those works, and that this note serves to rectify past mistakes of authorship attribution and prevent future mistakes.

Thought Questions (students consider while they read)

1. What does Charlotte Brontë, or Currer Bell, appreciate about her supporters? How might she have come to feel this way?

2. What messages does she have for her doubters?

3. What themes from the novel do you see in the Preface to the Second Edition?

4. Why might Brontë have written under the pseudonym of Currer Bell?

5. What is the stated purpose of the Note to the Third Edition, and why might Brontë have wanted to include it?

Vocabulary (in order of appearance)

Preface to the Second Edition: A preface to the first edition of "Jane Eyre" being unnecessary, I gave none: this second edition demands a few words both of acknowledgment and miscellaneous remark.

miscellaneous:

varied in type and from different types of sources

Preface to the Second Edition: To the Public, for the indulgent ear it has inclined to a plain tale with few pretensions.

indulgent:

generous, tolerant, forgiving

pretensions:

claims of being or having something

Preface to the Second Edition: To the Press, for the fair field its honest suffrage has opened to an obscure aspirant.

suffrage:

the right to vote, a vote of support, a prayer made on someone's behalf

obscure:

not well-known or well-understood

aspirant:

someone with a goal or ambition

Preface to the Second Edition: To my Publishers, for the aid their tact, their energy, their practical sense and

frank liberality have afforded an unknown and unrecommended Author.

tact:

a sense of what to say and do in order to not upset people

Preface to the Second Edition:I mean the timorous or carping few who doubt the tendency of such books as "Jane Eyre": in whose eyes whatever is unusual is wrong; whose ears detect in each protest against bigotry—that parent of crime—an insult to piety, that regent of God on earth.

timorous:

fearful, hesitant from a lack of confidence

Preface to the Second Edition: I mean the timorous or carping few who doubt the tendency of such books as "Jane Eyre:" in whose eyes whatever is unusual is wrong; whose ears detect in each protest against bigotry—that parent of crime—an insult to piety, that regent of God on earth.

carping:

complaining, critical in a fussy way

bigotry:

stubborn intolerance of others' differences

piety:

showing respect, showing duty and reverence to God

regent:

a holder of ruling power

Preface to the Second Edition: To attack the first is not to assail the last.

assail:

to attack or vigorously criticize

Preface to the Second Edition: These things and deeds are diametrically opposed: they are as distinct as is vice from virtue.

diametrically :

contrarily, exactly opposite

Preface to the Second Edition: Men too often confound them: they should not be confounded: appearance should not be mistaken for truth...

confound:

to mix up or confuse

Preface to the Second Edition: The world may not like to see these ideas dissevered, for it has been accustomed to blend them...

dissevered:

separated

Preface to the Second Edition: It may hate him who dares to scrutinise and expose—to rase the gilding, and show base metal under it—to penetrate the sepulchre, and reveal charnel relics: but hate as it will, it is indebted to him.

charnel:

suitable or used for receiving bodies and/or bones of the dead

Preface to the Second Edition: Ahab did not like Micaiah, because he never prophesied good concerning him, but evil; probably he liked the sycophant son of Chenaannah better

prophesied:

predicted

sycophant:

someone who attempts to win people's favor by flattering them

Preface to the Second Edition: There is a man in our own days whose words are not framed to tickle delicate ears: who, to my thinking, comes before the great ones of society, much as the son of Imlah came before the throned Kings of Judah and Israel; and who speaks truth as deep, with a power as prophet-like and as vital—a mien as dauntless and as daring

mien:

appearance or manner

dauntless:

fearless, unable to be intimidated

Preface to the Second Edition: ...but I think if some of those amongst whom he hurls the Greek fire of his sarcasm, and over whom he flashes the levin-brand of his denunciation, were to take his warnings in time—they or their seed might yet escape a fatal Rimoth-Gilead.

levin-brand:

a thunderbolt

Preface to the Second Edition: but I think if some of those amongst whom he hurls the Greek fire of his sarcasm, and over whom he flashes the levin-brand of his denunciation, were to take his warnings in time—they or their seed might yet escape a fatal Rimoth-Gilead.

denunciation:

open accusation or expression of disapproval

Preface to the Second Edition: Why have I alluded to this man?

alluded:

made a reference

Preface to the Second Edition: because I regard him as the first social regenerator of the day—as the very master of that working corps who would restore to rectitude the warped system of things;

rectitude:

the quality of being morally upright or correct in judgment

Preface to the Second Edition: Fielding could stoop on carrion, but Thackeray never does.

carrion:

dead and decaying flesh

Preface to the Second Edition: His wit is bright, his humour attractive, but both bear the same relation to his serious genius that the mere lambent sheet-lightning playing under the edge of the summer-cloud does to the electric death-spark hid in its womb.

lambent:

effortlessly light, flickering lightly

Note to the Third Edition: This explanation will serve to rectify mistakes which may already have been made, and to prevent future errors.

rectify:

to correct or set right

Additional Homework

1. Go online or to the library. Find answers to the following questions:

   1. What circumstances surrounded Charlotte Brontë's choice to use the pseudonym of Currer Bell?

   2. What was the purpose of the Note to the Third Edition?

Day 6 - Discussion of Thought Questions

1. What does Charlotte Brontë, or Currer Bell, appreciate about her supporters? How might she have come to feel this way?

Time:

5 minutes

Discussion:

She appreciates their enthusiasm, good sense, generous hearts, and open minds. Clearly, Brontë did not expect the kind of positive public response that her novel received, and she is delighted and gracious about it now that the book is going into a second printing.

2. What messages does she have for her doubters?

Time:

5 minutes

Discussion:

She tells them that an outward show of piety or morality is not the same thing as actually having these qualities. Neither is a rigid adherence to conventionality, self-righteousness, or dogma. While the world is often comfortable not examining beneath the surface of things, it ultimately appreciates those who do dig beneath the surface.

3. What themes from the novel do you see in the Preface to the Second Edition?

Time:

5 minutes

Discussion:

Brontë, like Jane, seems eager to distinguish between people she supports and people whose values she disagrees with. In touting Thackeray, she acts as Jane does, trying to cast light on the underappreciated and extraordinary. A complex understanding of morality, like Brontë shows here, is also a driving force of *Jane Eyre*.

4. Why might Brontë have written under the pseudonym of Currer Bell?

Time:

5 minutes

Discussion:

Some students will understand that the masculine name afforded a female author more freedom in a sexist era. Explore this idea, especially for a novel that relies so completely on the female point of view. Some may be aware that Brontë's sisters also wrote under pseudonyms, with corresponding initials—Emily Brontë was "Ellis Bell," Anne Brontë "Acton Bell"—and will believe that the sisters wanted a sense of unity even when they could not publish using their real names.

5. What is the stated purpose of the Note to the Third Edition, and why might Brontë have wanted to include it?

Time:

5 minutes

Discussion:

According to the author, it has been written to state that Currer Bell is the author of *Jane Eyre* and no other work of fiction, and to clarify any misunderstandings about Currer Bell being the author of any other works of fiction. Students may speculate regarding the confusion of authorship—some may know that Brontë's sisters wrote under assumed names, as well, and could understand that some readers might have thought all the "Bells" to be one person.

Day 6 - Short Answer Evaluation

1. Who is Currer Bell?

   _____

2. Why is Thackeray mentioned?

   _____

3. Who is thanked in the Preface to the Second Edition?

   _____

4. What is criticized in the Preface to the Second Edition?

   _____

5. What is explained in the Note to the Third Edition?

   _____

Answer Key

1. Currer Bell is Charlotte Brontë's pseudonym.
2. He is mentioned as an example of an author not afraid to dig beneath the surface and expose truths people might not want to face, and Currer Bell (or Charlotte Brontë) has dedicated the book to him.
3. The Public, Press, and Publishers are thanked.
4. People who put on the outward appearance of virtue without having virtue inside are criticized, as are people unwilling to look below the surface of people or situations.
5. It is explained that Currer Bell is the author of Jane Eyre and no other work of fiction, and that other authors should be given credit for work they have written that has been attributed to Currer Bell.

Day 6 - Crossword Puzzle

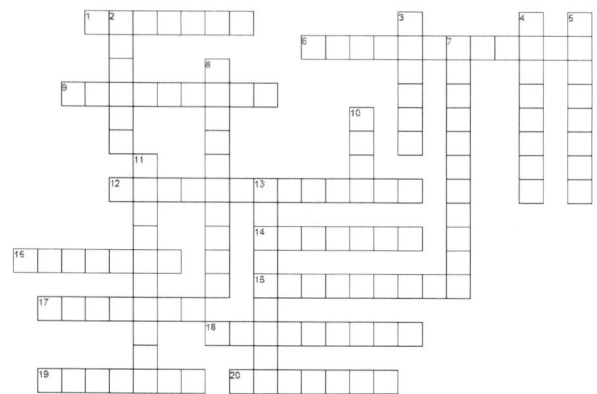

ACROSS

1. Dead and decaying flesh
6. Claims of being or having something
9. The second edition of Jane Eyre is dedicated to
   _____
12. Contrarily, exactly opposite
14. Complaining, critical in a fussy way
15. Suitable or used for receiving bodies and/or bones of the dead
16. Generous, tolerant, forgiving
17. Effortlessly light, flickering lightly
18. Fearless, unable to be intimidated
19. Made a reference
20. To correct or set right

DOWN

2. To attack or vigorously criticize
3. A holder of ruling power
4. To mix up or confuse
5. Someone with a goal or ambition
7. A levin-brand is a _____.
8. Predicted
10. Jane Eyre was written under the pseudonym of Currer
    _____
11. Separated
13. The quality of being morally upright or correct in judgment

Crossword Puzzle Answer Key

ACROSS

1. Dead and decaying flesh
6. Claims of being or having something
9. The second edition of Jane Eyre is dedicated to
   _____
12. Contrarily, exactly opposite
14. Complaining, critical in a fussy way
15. Suitable or used for receiving bodies and/or bones of the dead
16. Generous, tolerant, forgiving
17. Effortlessly light, flickering lightly
18. Fearless, unable to be intimidated
19. Made a reference
20. To correct or set right

DOWN

2. To attack or vigorously criticize
3. A holder of ruling power
4. To mix up or confuse
5. Someone with a goal or ambition
7. A levin-brand is a _____.
8. Predicted
10. Jane Eyre was written under the pseudonym of Currer
    _____
11. Separated
13. The quality of being morally upright or correct in judgment

Day 6 - Vocabulary Quiz

Terms

1. _____ indulgent
2. _____ miscellaneous
3. _____ pretensions
4. _____ suffrage
5. _____ obscure
6. _____ tact
7. _____ aspirant
8. _____ timorous
9. _____ regent
10. _____ confound
11. _____ prophesied
12. _____ sycophant
13. _____ dauntless
14. _____ mien
15. _____ alluded
16. _____ denunciation
17. _____ bigotry
18. _____ assail
19. _____ dissevered
20. _____ rectitude

Answers

A. someone who attempts to win people's favor by flattering them
B. the quality of being morally upright or correct in judgment
C. not well-known or well-understood
D. predicted
E. a sense of what to say and do in order to not upset people
F. fearless, unable to be intimidated
G. separated
H. to attack or vigorously criticize
I. a holder of ruling power
J. someone with a goal or ambition
K. to mix up or confuse
L. the right to vote, a vote of support, a prayer made on someone's behalf
M. claims of being or having something
N. fearful, hesitant from a lack of confidence
O. appearance or manner
P. varied in type and from different types of sources
Q. stubborn intolerance of others' differences
R. generous, tolerant, forgiving
S. made a reference
T. open accusation or expression of disapproval

Answer Key

1. R indulgent: generous, tolerant, forgiving
2. P miscellaneous: varied in type and from different types of sources
3. M pretensions: claims of being or having something
4. L suffrage: the right to vote, a vote of support, a prayer made on someone's behalf
5. C obscure: not well-known or well-understood
6. E tact: a sense of what to say and do in order to not upset people
7. J aspirant: someone with a goal or ambition
8. N timorous: fearful, hesitant from a lack of confidence
9. I regent: a holder of ruling power
10. K confound: to mix up or confuse
11. D prophesied: predicted
12. A sycophant: someone who attempts to win people's favor by flattering them
13. F dauntless: fearless, unable to be intimidated
14. O mien: appearance or manner
15. S alluded: made a reference
16. T denunciation: open accusation or expression of disapproval
17. Q bigotry: stubborn intolerance of others' differences
18. H assail: to attack or vigorously criticize
19. G dissevered: separated
20. B rectitude: the quality of being morally upright or correct in judgment

Day 6 - Classroom Activities

1. Pseudonym Think-Pair-Share

Kind of Activity:

Group Discussion

Objective:

In this activity, students will consider possible pseudonyms for themselves as writers.

Common Core Standards:

CCSS.ELA-LITERACY.RL.11-12.10; CCSS.ELA-Literacy.SL.11-12.1

Time:

15 minutes

Structure:

As seen in the readings for today's class, Charlotte Brontë wrote *Jane Eyre* under the pseudonym, or pen name (a name a writer uses instead of the writer's own name), of Currer Bell. In this activity, students will consider what they would choose for pseudonyms for themselves.

1. Students should, individually, take a few minutes to choose a pseudonym. They should write down their chosen pseudonyms along with brief explanations of the reasons behind the chosen pseudonyms.

2. In pairs, students should discuss their pseudonym choices and the reasons behind them.

3. After discussing in pairs, the class should reconvene as a whole and each student should present to the class his or her partner's choice of pseudonym and the reason behind that choice.

Ideas for Differentiated Instruction:

Before having students decide on their own pseudonyms, the teacher can discuss with the class other authors' choices of pseudonyms. Besides Charlotte Brontë's choice of Currer Bell, some other examples of authors' pseudonyms are:

Pseudonym Author

Acton Bell Anne Brontë

Ellis Bell Emily Brontë

George Eliot Mary Ann Evans

George Orwell Eric Arthur Blair

J.K. Rowling Joanne Kathleen Rowling

P.L. Travers Helen Goff

Lemony Snicket Daniel Handler

Assessment Ideas:

The teacher can collect what students have written down about their pseudonym choices and the reasons behind those choices and grade the assignments for completion.

2. Writing a Story Using a Pseudonym

Kind of Activity:

Individual Writing

Objective:

Students will write stories under their pseudonyms.

Common Core Standards:

CCSS.ELA-LITERACY.RL.11-12.10; CCSS.ELA-Literacy.W.11-12.3; CCSS.ELA-Literacy.W.11-12.6

Time:

45 minutes

Structure:

1. At the beginning of class, the students should write for ten minutes, coming up with as many story ideas as possible that they might write using their pseudonyms instead of their real names.

2. Students should choose one of their story ideas and expand it into a full story.

3. When finished, students should upload their stories to a class blog or document-sharing site along with a brief explanation of their pseudonyms. Why did they choose this particular pseudonym, and what impact did it have on their writing? Did "Dante Rice" write stories that were different from those that "David Jordan" would write? Why?

Ideas for Differentiated Instruction:

As an extended activity, students can trade pseudonyms and can write stories using their new names.

Assessment Ideas:

The stories can be collected and graded for:

-grammar and mechanics

-effort and creativity

Final Paper

Essay Questions

1. How does *Jane Eyre* comment on the purpose(s) of education?

2. Choose an event in Jane's life that seems to have has an impact on her. Describe the event and explain the effect that it has on her.

3. To whom does Jane turn for mentorship in the novel? What lesson(s) does she learn from her mentor(s)?

4. What personal values does Jane hold? Do these values stay consistent throughout the novel?

5. How do descriptions of weather complement and/or contrast with the narrative of events in the novel?

6. What do you think is a major theme in *Jane Eyre*? How is this theme brought out over the course of the novel?

7. Is there a point in *Jane Eyre* when a character makes a mistake? What is the mistake and would could the character have done differently?

Advice on research sources

A. School or community library

Ask your reference librarian for help locating books on the following subjects:

* *Jane Eyre*

* Charlotte Brontë

* the Victorian Era

B. Personal experience

Have you ever felt alone and longed for personal connection? Have you ever been unfairly accused of something? Have you ever had an influential mentor? Have you ever had an obstacle stand between you and something you wanted? Have regrets or mistakes from the past ever held you back in the present?

Grading rubric for essays

Content (75%):

* Accuracy: does the essay use the facts of the novel correctly?

* Use of evidence: does the essay include textual evidence to support its original arguments?

* Addresses the question: does the essay answer the topic question posed?

* Completeness: does the essay present a complete argument? Does it go into depth on its main points?

* Uses literary concepts: does the essay make its argument using not only emotional persuasion, but also literary ideas learned in class?

* Subtlety: does the essay address complex and sensitive subjects with understanding and nuance?

* Argument: does the argument make sense? Is it successfully presented? Is it original?

Style (25%):

* Words: are the words in the essay spelled correctly? Are the word choices appropriate to the topic?

* Sentences: do the sentences utilize Standard English grammar? Are punctuation marks used appropriately?

* Paragraphs: does each paragraph contain a topic sentence? Does each make a coherent point?

* Essay structure: does the essay contain an introduction, three or more body paragraphs that explore distinct ideas or examples, and a conclusion?

Answer Key for Final Essays

Remember that essays about literature should not be graded with a cookie-cutter approach whereby specific words or ideas are required. See the grading rubric above for a variety of criteria to use in assessing answers to the essay questions. This answer key thus functions as a store of ideas for students who need additional guidance in framing their answers.

1. How does *Jane Eyre* comment on the purpose(s) of education?

Students may note that, for women in the Victorian Era, education provides both a set of accomplishments with which to shine in social situations and potentially attract a suitable husband and also a set of skills and body of knowledge to rely on to become a teacher or governess in order to be able to survive in the world independently. Students may also consider the various educational goals held by teachers and administrators at Lowood. Students may also consider what Jane learns as a teacher at the girls' school opened by St. John Rivers in Morton, and of the way that Jane assesses Adèle's schooling, both while acting as her governess and at the end of the novel.

2. Choose an event in Jane's life that seems to have has an impact on her. Describe the event and explain the effect that it has on her.

A strong essay will explain the event in detail, using textual evidence, and analyze Jane's perspective and response from several angles. Students may, for instance, choose Jane's inheritance of twenty thousand pounds from her uncle. This event sets Jane free financially, making her able to completely make her own choices in life. It also makes her able to help Diana, Mary, and St. John Rivers, and able to approach Mr. Rochester on terms of greater equality than she could when she worked as his governess.

3. To whom does Jane turn for mentorship in the novel? What lesson(s) does she learn from her mentor(s)?

One mentor students may choose is Miss Temple. She functions as a person to whom Jane can look up and also go to for advice, first when Jane is a student and later when Jane is a fellow teacher at Lowood. Another possible choice could be Helen Burns, who helps Jane through her initial rough adjustment period at Lowood, or Mrs. Fairfax, whose kindness supports Jane in her early days at Thornfield Hall. A strong essay should analyze what Jane is looking for in a mentor, and to what degree the mentor in question makes those qualities available.

4. What personal values does Jane hold? Do these values stay consistent throughout the novel?

Students may, for instance, focus on Jane's honesty which stays pretty much constant through the novel, even in cases where lying may be more diplomatic, such as her response to Mr. Rochester's question to her about whether he is handsome. This honesty is questioned by Mr. Brocklehurst, but later corroborated by Mr. Lloyd, the apothecary who takes care of Jane after her traumatic experience in the red-room. Students may also focus on Jane's desire for real love and human connection. She is grateful for relatives who care about her, so she helps Mary, Diana, and St. John financially when she has the chance. She also refuses St. John's marriage proposal because she does not love him. She also refuses Mr. Rochester's first proposal, not because she doesn't love him, but she does not want to live in the situation that he has put her in, and wrenches herself away to find a life for herself on her own. Independence is another possible value that can be discussed, as Jane's leaving Thornfield after finding out about Mr. Rochester's wife also shows.

5. How do descriptions of weather complement and/or contrast with the narrative of events in the novel?

Students may note that descriptions of weather and landscapes, when paired with the listing of months, can denote the passing of time in the novel. Students may also write that there are times when the weather seems to mirror and/or Jane's internal state and/or events going on around her, and also times when Jane's internal state and/or events are described metaphorically using weather imagery.

6. What do you think is a major theme in *Jane Eyre*? How is this theme brought out over the course of the novel?

A strong essay will explain the theme and their reasons for selecting it, and then utilize multiple examples from different points in the text to strengthen the argument. Students may, for instance, write on theme of Inner vs. Outer Beauty and consider the ways in which Jane, while often outwardly overlooked, has an inner beauty that shines through, as opposed to Blanche Ingram, whose inner lack of beauty can sometimes overshadow her outer attractiveness.

7. Is there a point in *Jane Eyre* when a character makes a mistake? What is the mistake and would could the character have done differently?

Essays should pinpoint a particular incident and analyze the repercussions of the character's choice throughout the text. Students may write, for example, that Mr. Rochester makes a mistake by getting married in the first place without really getting to know his potential bride, or they may write that he makes a mistake by proposing to Jane when he is already married, without even telling Jane what he is doing. These choices obviously have a significant impact on the story.

Final Exam

Multiple Choice

Circle the letter corresponding to the best answer.

1. Which language does Jane speak fluently?

    A. German
    B. Italian
    C. Spanish
    D. French

2. The author of Jane Eyre wrote under which pen name?

    A. Currer Bell
    B. Acton Bell
    C. Jane Austen
    D. Anne Shirley

3. At the beginning of the novel, Jane is living in the home of:

    A. Mrs. Eyre
    B. Mrs. Reed
    C. Mrs. Fairfax
    D. Mrs. Bell

4. Jane takes a job as a governess in the home of:

    A. Mr. Fielding
    B. Mr. Lynn
    C. Colonel Dent
    D. Mr. Rochester

5. Another word for a pen name is:

    A. pseudonym
    B. synechdoche

C. metronome

D. antonym

6. What are the names of John Reed's sisters?

A. Eliza and Georgiana

B. Charlotte and Emily

C. Grace and Blanche

D. Leah and Lynn

7. What school does Jane attend?

A. Fairfax

B. Thornfield

C. Lowood

D. Fielding

8. The second edition of Jane Eyre is dedicated to whom?

A. Thackeray

B. Fielding

C. Bell

D. Austen

9. At one point, Jane thinks that Mr. Rochester might marry:

A. Georgiana

B. Miss Ingram

C. Miss Temple

D. Diana

10. What are the names of St. John's sisters?

A. Charlotte and Anne

B. Blanche and Sarah

C. Emily and Bessie

D. Diana and Mary

11. Adèle is the daughter of:

A. Céline Varens

B. Georgiana Reed

C. John Eyre

D. Diana Ingram

12. When Jane first meets Mr. Rochester, what does she do?

A. helps him onto his horse

B. ignores him

C. leaves him stranded

D. walks with him to mail a letter

13. What is the name of Mr. Rochester's dog?

A. Pilot

B. Rover

C. Max

D. Spot

14. Grace Poole works in the house of:

A. Mrs. Reed

B. Miss Ingram

C. Mr. Brocklehurst

D. Mr. Rochester

15. In order to clear Jane of any accusations, Miss Temple writes to:

A. Mr. Rochester

B. Mrs. Fairfax

C. Miss Ingram

D. Mr. Lloyd

16. Who comes to visit Jane right before Jane leaves Lowood to go work as a governess?

A. Bessie

B. Leah

C. Georgiana

D. Eliza

17. Mr. Lloyd suggests to Jane that she could:

A. work at Thornfield as a governess
B. marry Mr. Rochester
C. go to school
D. walk to Hay to post a letter

18. What disease breaks out at Lowood?

A. Salmonella
B. Typhus Fever
C. Influenza
D. Malaria

19. What is Helen Burns reading when Jane first meets her?

A. Wuthering Heights
B. Great Expectations
C. Persuasion
D. Rasselas

20. Which teacher constantly punishes and criticizes Helen Burns?

A. Miss Temple
B. Miss Scatcherd
C. Mrs. Reed
D. Mr. Pumblechook

Short Answer

1. What reason is given for the dedication to the second edition to *Jane Eyre?*

   _____

2. What prompts Jane to consider leaving her teaching position at Lowood?

   _____

3. Why does Miss Temple provide bread and butter for the students on Jane's first full day of classes at Lowood?

   _____

4. Compare the way the students at Lowood are dressed with the way that Mr. Brocklehurst's wife and daughters are dressed.

   _____

5. Where does Jane spend her school vacations?

   _____

6. Who is Mary Ann Wilson?

   _____

7. What does Mr. Brocklehurst accuse Jane of in front of teachers and students at Lowood?

   _____

8. How does Mrs. Reed treat Jane when Jane is living in Mrs. Reed's home?

   _____

9. What information does Mr. Briggs reveal?

_____

10. What happens to Thornfield Hall?

_____

Vocabulary Questions

Terms

1. _____ lamentable
2. _____ assiduity
3. _____ corroborate
4. _____ absolved
5. _____ confabulate
6. _____ acrimony
7. _____ tirade
8. _____ bairn
9. _____ affable
10. _____ evasive
11. _____ perfidy
12. _____ ameliorated
13. _____ indulgent
14. _____ confound
15. _____ rectify
16. _____ miscellaneous
17. _____ counterfeit
18. _____ ponderous
19. _____ puerile
20. _____ scoundrel

Answers

A. a long and angry speech
B. made something bad, such as a problem, better
C. seeking to avoid something
D. bitterness, hostility, ill feeling
E. heavy, cumbersome
F. varied in type and from different types of sources
G. freed from guilt, obligation, or blame
H. in fraudulent imitation
I. have a conversation
J. to mix up or confuse
K. a dishonest or unprincipled person
L. to correct or set right
M. a child
N. validate, confirm, give support to
O. betrayal of faith or trust
P. careful and constant attention or effort
Q. generous, tolerant, forgiving
R. easy to talk to, friendly
S. regrettably bad, unfortunate, full of sorrow
T. childish, immature

Short Essays

1. What role does visual art play in Jane's life?

_____

_____

_____

_____

_____

2. Compare St. John Rivers with Mr. Rochester.

_____

_____

_____

_____

_____

3. Jane tells Mr. Rochester, "I am no bird; and no net ensnares me..." What does she mean? How is this true of Jane throughout the novel?

_____

_____

_____

_____

Final Exam Answer Key

Multiple Choice

1. **(D)** French
2. **(A)** Currer Bell
3. **(B)** Mrs. Reed
4. **(D)** Mr. Rochester
5. **(A)** pseudonym
6. **(A)** Eliza and Georgiana
7. **(C)** Lowood
8. **(A)** Thackeray
9. **(B)** Miss Ingram
10. **(D)** Diana and Mary
11. **(A)** Céline Varens
12. **(A)** helps him onto his horse
13. **(A)** Pilot
14. **(D)** Mr. Rochester
15. **(D)** Mr. Lloyd
16. **(A)** Bessie
17. **(C)** go to school
18. **(B)** Typhus Fever
19. **(D)** Rasselas
20. **(B)** Miss Scatcherd

Short Answer

1. The second edition is dedicated to Thackeray because he exposes the world's hypocrisies and looks beneath the façades many people are comfortable hiding behind, which much of the world is happy to accept.
2. Miss Temple gets married and leaves Lowood and, at first, Jane feels rootless without her mentor. Then, this rootless leads to a feeling of openness to new opportunities.
3. The students have to eat burned porridge for breakfast.
4. The students at Lowood are dressed in plain and unflattering uniforms, whereas Mr. Brocklehurst's wife and daughters are dressed lavishly.
5. She spends her vacations at Lowood.
6. Mary Ann Wilson is a friend of Jane's with whom Jane spends time during Lowood's typhus fever outbreak, as Helen Burns is also sick during this time, but with consumption, not typhus fever.
7. Mr. Brocklehurst accuses Jane of being a liar.
8. Mrs. Reed is dismissive and critical of Jane, discouraging her children from associating with Jane.

9. He announces that Mr. Rochester is already married, so he cannot marry Jane.
10. Bertha Mason sets Thornfield Hall on fire and it burns down.

Vocabulary Questions

1. S lamentable: regrettably bad, unfortunate, full of sorrow
2. P assiduity: careful and constant attention or effort
3. N corroborate: validate, confirm, give support to
4. G absolved: freed from guilt, obligation, or blame
5. I confabulate: have a conversation
6. D acrimony: bitterness, hostility, ill feeling
7. A tirade: a long and angry speech
8. M bairn: a child
9. R affable: easy to talk to, friendly
10. C evasive: seeking to avoid something
11. O perfidy: betrayal of faith or trust
12. B ameliorated: made something bad, such as a problem, better
13. Q indulgent: generous, tolerant, forgiving
14. J confound: to mix up or confuse
15. L rectify: to correct or set right
16. F miscellaneous: varied in type and from different types of sources
17. H counterfeit: in fraudulent imitation
18. E ponderous: heavy, cumbersome
19. T puerile: childish, immature
20. K scoundrel: a dishonest or unprincipled person

Short Essays

1. For Jane, visual art is an outlet, a source of pride in her accomplishment, and a way to connect with others. For instance, her art inspires conversation and facilitated points of connection between her and Mr. Rochester, Eliza Reed, Georgiana Reed, Diana Rivers, and Mary Rivers. It also seems to serve as an escape for her, something she does to clarify her thoughts when she is confused in other ways, as when she draws the portrait of Mr. Rochester.

2. Both men are extreme characters, and both see interesting things in Jane. Mr. Rochester falls into a dissolute lifestyle in response to the deterioration of his marriage. St. John, on the other hand, is very strict with himself and with others. St. John helps to facilitate Jane's independence by offering her a teaching position at his school, and she returns the favor when she can by sharing her inheritance with him and his sisters. He does not love her, but proposes to her as a rational calculation that she can be helpful to him in his missionary work in India. Mr. Rochester, on the other hand, proposes to

Jane because his passion for her overwhelms him, in contrast with St. John, who proposes to Jane precisely because he feels no passion for her.

3. Jane tells this to Mr. Rochester when tells her that he is going to marry Blanche Ingram, as an expression of her independence. Jane strives for independence throughout the novel, reaching into her supply of inner resources in order to make her way in the world. Rather than stay with Mr. Rochester, for instance, in a situation which is untenable, she leaves and throws herself on the mercy of the world. She eventually is taken in by Diana, Mary, and St. John Rivers (later discovered to be Jane's cousins) and, while grateful for their kindness, also wants to be as independent of it as possible. St. John helps her with this by employing her as a teacher at the school he has just opened. Jane becomes even more independent when she inherits money from her uncle, who is also the uncle of St. John, Mary, and Diana, and uses her newfound wealth to help her cousins find financial independence, as well.

Lesson Plans

GrdeSaver™

Getting you the grade since 1999™

Other Lesson Plans from GradeSaver™

12 Angry Men
1984
A Christmas Carol
A Doll's House
A Farewell to Arms
Alexander Hamilton
Alice in Wonderland
Allen Ginsberg's
    Poetry
All Quiet on the
    Western Front
Americanah
Animal Farm
An Inspector Calls
Anna Karenina
Antigone
A Raisin in the Sun
Arcadia
Around the World in
    80 Days
A Separate Peace
As I Lay Dying

A Streetcar Named
    Desire
A Tale of Two Cities
A Thousand
    Splendid Suns
Atonement
A View From the
    Bridge
Beloved
Beowulf
Between the World
    and Me
Bhagavad-Gita
Black Boy
Bless Me, Ultima
Brave New World
Breakfast at
    Tiffany's
Bury My Heart at
    Wounded Knee
Call of the Wild
Cannery Row
Catching Fire

Cathedral
Cat's Cradle
Ceremony
Christopher
    Marlowe's Poems
Connecticut Yankee
    in King Arthur's
    Court
Death of a Salesman
Desire Under the
    Elms
Do Androids Dream
    of Electric Sheep?
Doctor Faustus
    (Marlowe)
Dr. Jekyll and Mr.
    Hyde
Dubliners
Emily Dickinson's
    Collected Poems
Emma
Ender's Game
Equus

For our full list of over 300 Study Guides, Quizzes, Lesson Plans
Sample College Application Essays, Literature Essays and E-texts, visit:

www.gradesaver.com

Lesson Plans

GradeSaver™

Getting you the grade since 1999™

Other Lesson Plans from GradeSaver™

Esperanza Rising
Everyman: Morality Play
Fahrenheit 451
Fangirl
Flannery O'Connor's Stories
Flowers for Algernon
For Colored Girls Who Have Considered Suicide When the Rainbow Is Enuf
Founding Brothers
Frankenstein
Franny and Zooey
Gone Girl
Go Set a Watchman
Go Tell it On the Mountain
Great Expectations
Gulliver's Travels

Hamlet
Heart of Darkness
Holes
House of Mirth
House on Mango Street
I Am Malala
I Know Why the Caged Bird Sings
Incidents in the Life of a Slave Girl
In Cold Blood
In the Time of the Butterflies
Into the Wild
Invisible Man
Island of the Blue Dolphins
Jane Eyre
John Donne: Poems
Jorge Borges: Short Stories

Journey to the Center of the Earth
Julius Caesar
Juno and the Paycock
Kate Chopin's Short Stories
Kindred
King Lear
Last of the Mohicans
Leaves of Grass
Let the Circle be Unbroken
Life of Pi
Little Women
Looking for Alaska
Lord Byron's Poems
Lord Jim
Lord of the Flies
Macbeth

For our full list of over 300 Study Guides, Quizzes, Lesson Plans
Sample College Application Essays, Literature Essays and E-texts, visit:

www.gradesaver.com

GrAdeSaver™

Getting you the grade since 1999™

Other Lesson Plans from GradeSaver™

Master Harold...
And the Boys
MAUS
Medea
Merchant of Venice
Middlemarch
Middlesex
Mockingjay
Montana 1948
Mother Courage and
Her Children
Mrs. Dalloway
My Antonia
My Brilliant Friend
Mythology
Never Let Me Go
Night
Oedipus Rex or
Oedipus the King
Of Mice and Men
Oliver Twist
One Flew Over the
Cuckoo's Nest

One Hundred Years
of Solitude
O Pioneers
Oroonoko
Oryx and Crake
Othello
Our Town
Paper Towns
Percy Shelley:
Poems
Persepolis: The
Story of a
Childhood
Poe's Poetry
Pride and Prejudice
Purple Hibiscus
Pygmalion
Reading Lolita in
Tehran
Rhinoceros
Rip Van Winkle and
Other Stories
Robert Frost: Poems

Robinson Crusoe
Roll of Thunder,
Hear My Cry
Romeo and Juliet
Roots
Rosencrantz and
Guildenstern Are
Dead
Shakespeare's
Sonnets
Short Stories of
Ernest
Hemingway
Siddhartha
Songs of Innocence
and of Experience
Speak
Station Eleven
Sula
Tess of the
D'Urbervilles

For our full list of over 300 Study Guides, Quizzes, Lesson Plans
Sample College Application Essays, Literature Essays and E-texts, visit:

www.gradesaver.com

Lesson Plans

GrⱭdeSaver™

Getting you the grade since 1999™

Other Lesson Plans from GradeSaver™

The Absolutely True Diary of a Part-Time Indian

The Adventures of Huckleberry Finn

The Adventures of Tom Sawyer

The Alchemist (Coelho)

The American

The Autobiography of Benjamin Franklin

The Awakening

The Bell Jar

The Bloody Chamber

The Book Thief

The Boy in the Striped Pajamas

The Brief Wondrous Life of Oscar Wao

The Canterbury Tales

The Catcher in the Rye

The Cherry Orchard

The Chosen

The Color Purple

The Count of Monte Cristo

The Crucible

The Curious Incident of the Dog in the Night-time

The Diary of a Young Girl by Anne Frank

The English Patient

The Epic of Gilgamesh

The Fault in Our Stars

The Girl on the Train

The Giver

The Glass Menagerie

The God of Small Things

The Golden Compass

The Grapes of Wrath

The Great Gatsby

The Guest

The Handmaid's Tale

The Heart Is a Lonely Hunter

The Help

The History Boys

The Hobbit

The Hot Zone

The Hound of the Baskervilles

For our full list of over 300 Study Guides, Quizzes, Lesson Plans
Sample College Application Essays, Literature Essays and E-texts, visit:

www.gradesaver.com

Lesson Plans

GradeSaver™

Getting you the grade since 1999™

Other Lesson Plans from GradeSaver™

The House of the
Spirits
The Hunger Games
The Importance of
Being Earnest
Their Eyes Were
Watching God
The Jungle
The Jungle Book
The Kite Runner
The Legend of
Sleepy Hollow
The Lone Ranger
and Tonto
Fistfight in
Heaven
The Long Goodbye
The Love Song of J.
Alfred Prufrock
The Martian
Chronicles
The Master and
Margarita

The Maze Runner
The Member of the
Wedding
The Metamorphosis
The Moonlit Road
and Other Ghost
and Horror
Stories
The Namesake
The Necklace
The Odyssey
The Old Man and
the Sea
The Once and
Future King
The Outsiders
The Overcoat
The Pearl
The Perks of Being
a Wallflower
The Poisonwood
Bible
The Quiet American

The Red Badge of
Courage
The Rime of the
Ancient Mariner
The Road
The Scarlet Letter
The Seagull
The Secret Life of
Bees
The Story of My
Life
The Stranger
The Tempest
The Things They
Carried
The Tortilla Curtain
The Turn of the
Screw
The Waste Land
The Wave
The Woman Warrior
The Wonderful
Wizard of Oz

For our full list of over 300 Study Guides, Quizzes, Lesson Plans
Sample College Application Essays, Literature Essays and E-texts, visit:

www.gradesaver.com

GradeSaver™

Getting you the grade since 1999™

Other Lesson Plans from GradeSaver™

The Yellow
   Wallpaper
Things Fall Apart
Thirteen Reasons
   Why
To Build a Fire
To Kill a
   Mockingbird
Topdog/Underdog
Top Girls
To the Lighthouse

Touching Spirit Bear
Trifles
Uncle Tom's Cabin
Waiting for Godot
Waiting for Lefty
Walden
Washington Square
Watership Down
Weep Not, Child
We Need New
   Names

White Teeth
Wide Sargasso Sea
Wonder
Wordsworth's
   Poetical Works
Wuthering Heights
Young Goodman
   Brown and Other
   Hawthorne Short
   Stories

For our full list of over 300 Study Guides, Quizzes, Lesson Plans
Sample College Application Essays, Literature Essays and E-texts, visit:

www.gradesaver.com